16 designs in Natural Silk Aran,
Cashcotton 4ply, Cashsoft DK &
Cashsoft Baby DK by Martin Storey

Pregnancy is a magical time
and children are our promise
to the future. In Classic Mother
and Baby we celebrate both
pregnancy and the early years
of your baby's life. Wrap
yourself in delicately patterned
shawls and cardigans that
flatter your figure. Snuggle
your baby in beautiful blankets
and warm slipovers. Watch as
they grow into cute ballet
wraps and Fairisle cardigans.

Martin

the designs

Candy coloured tops, traditional fairisles, lacy motifs
and flattering shapes for the mother to be.

SIZE KEY: ▲   Size S - XL   +   Accessory (Refer to pattern page)

Bonbon

A riot of sweet colours in this dolman cardigan with bobble and embroidery detail. Knitted in Cashsoft DK, shown here in Sweet, Bloom, Lime & Mirage. Pattern instructions page 58

Alphabet Blanket

This timeless, heirloom blanket is in an
intarsia alphabet stitch and decorated with
a delightful cable border. Knitted in Cashsoft
DK shown here in Tape, Kingfisher, Cashew,
Donkey, Lichen, Navy & Bloom. Pattern
instructions page 52

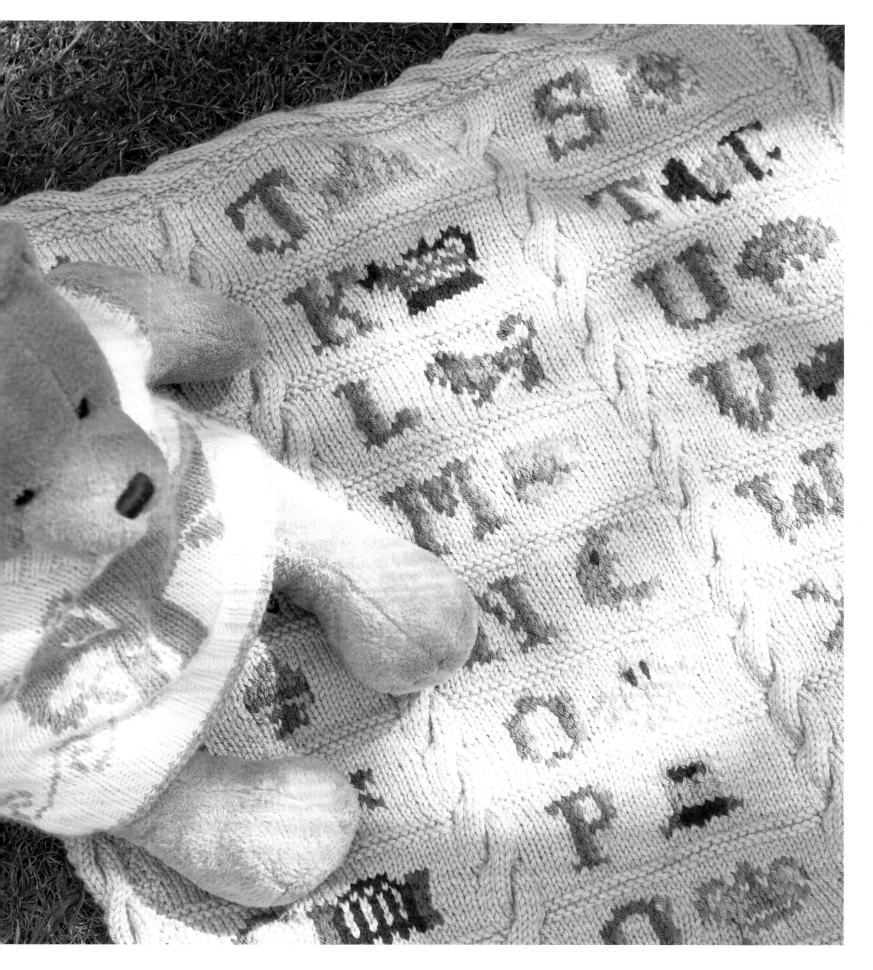

The elephant, so big and grey
Is gentle as can be.
He's careful where he puts his feet,
and tiptoes de-li-cate-ly

Zoo

An adorable slipover with a friendly elephant motif. Knitted in Cashcotton 4 ply shown here in Cream, Cork & Seafoam. Pattern instructions page 86

Angelica

Our rib cardigan has a deep lace trim detail and pretty cable borders. Knitted in Cashsoft DK, Bloom shown here with Liquorice. Pattern instructions page 54

Liquorice Jacket
A traditional wide striped jacket with pockets.

Liquorice Beanie
Keep warm with this two colour stripe beanie.
Both knitted in Natural Silk Aran shown here
in Black & Flax. Pattern instructions
pages 70 & 72

May
Our shrug has a lovely bobble and cable texture and fastens elegantly with knitted ties. Knitted in Cashsoft DK shown here in Tape. Pattern instructions page 76

Mary, Mary quite contrary
How does your garden grow?
With silver bells and cockle shells
And pretty maids all in a row.

Betony
This lacy bolero is just perfect for the grown-
up little girl with its pretty ribbon ████████
around borders and cuffs. K███████████████
DK shown here in Bella Donna. Pattern
instructions page 56

Hazel

Our garter stitch jacket with its elegant, deep cable and rib collar, fastens with a pin at the neck. Knitted in Natural Silk Aran Palm Leaf, shown above with Butterscotch. Pattern instructions page 62

Lollipop

A lovely ballet wrap in a floral lace stitch for a baby on the move. Knitted in Cashcotton 4 ply shown here in Citron. Pattern instructions page 74

Hemlock

This versatile waistcoat in a lace cable stitch
has a garter yoke and is so flattering. Knitted
in Natural Silk Aran shown here in Charm
Pattern instructions page 64

Butterscotch
Stay snug in a raglan sleeve
sweater knitted in moss stitch
finished off with a smart polo
collar. Knitted in Natural Silk Aran
shown here & right in Palm Leaf,
above in cream. Pattern
instructions page 60

Nougat
What every baby needs, a smart double-breasted cardigan in a horizontal rib.
Knitted in Cashsoft DK shown here in Mist.
Pattern instructions page 78

Sampler Blanket
Wonderful squares of texture in a vintage star design make up this patchwork blanket. Knitted in Cashsoft DK shown here in Cream.
Pattern instructions page 73

Penny Jacket & Penny Beanie
So wearable. This classic cardigan & beanie
come in a colourful diamond and bobble
stitch. Knitted in Baby Cashsoft DK shown
here in Horseradish, Ballad Blue, Sweet,
Bloom, Glacier, Lime & Mirage. Pattern
instructions pages 83 & 84

Penny Gilet

This sophisticated shawl collar gilet is knitted
in a diamond & bobble stitch and fastens with
a pin at the waist. Knitted in Cashsoft DK
shown here in Savannah, Kingfisher, Cashew,
Poison, Mist, Navy & Lichen. Pattern
instructions page 80

Honeysuckle
The timeless texture of a diamond lace
and bead stitch adorn this ballet wrap.
Knitted in Cashcotton 4 ply shown here in
Peppermint. Pattern instructions page 66

Apples on the tree
Apples on the tree
Green and red and golden ones
And some to have for tea.

Humbug Hood

Take the chill off a summer evening in this lovely hoodie with pouch pockets and a drawstring hem. Knitted in Natural Silk Aran shown here in Flax. Pattern instructions page 68

True friends forever
Through thick and thin
Explorers together
Till mum calls us in.

Tension

Obtaining the correct tension is perhaps the single factor which can make the difference between a successful garment and a disastrous one. It controls both the shape and size of an article, so any variation, however slight, can distort the finished garment. Different designers feature in our books and it is **their** tension, given at the **start** of each pattern, which you must match. We recommend that you knit a square in pattern and/or stocking stitch (depending on the pattern instructions) of perhaps 5 - 10 more stitches and 5 - 10 more rows than those given in the tension note. Mark out the central 10cm square with pins. If you have too many stitches to 10cm try again using thicker needles, if you have too few stitches to 10cm try again using finer needles. Once you have achieved the correct tension your garment will be knitted to the measurements indicated in the size diagram shown at the end of the pattern.

Sizing and Size Diagram Note

The instructions are given for the smallest size. Where they vary, work the figures in brackets for the larger sizes. **One set of figures refers to all sizes.** Included with most patterns in this magazine is a **'size diagram'**, or sketch of the finished garment and its dimensions. The size diagram shows the finished width of the garment at the under-arm point, and it is this measurement that the knitter should choose first; a useful tip is to measure one of your own garments which is a comfortable fit. Having chosen a size based on width, look at the corresponding length for that size; if you are not happy with the total length which we recommend, adjust your own garment before beginning your armhole shaping - any adjustment after this point will mean that your sleeve will not fit into your garment easily - don't forget to take your adjustment into account if there is any side seam shaping. Finally, look at the sleeve length; the size diagram shows the finished sleeve measurement, taking into account any top-arm insertion length. Measure your body between the centre of your neck and your wrist, this measurement should correspond to half the garment width plus the sleeve length. Again, your sleeve length may be adjusted, but remember to take into consideration your sleeve increases if you do adjust the length - you must increase more frequently than the pattern states to shorten your sleeve, less frequently to lengthen it.

Chart Note

Many of the patterns in the book are worked from charts. Each square on a chart represents a stitch and each line of squares a row of knitting. Each colour used is given a different letter and these are shown in the **materials** section, or in the **key** alongside the chart of each pattern. When working from the charts, read odd rows (K) from right to left and even rows (P) from left to right, unless otherwise stated.

Knitting with colour

There are two main methods of working colour into a knitted fabric: Intarsia and Fairisle techniques. The first method produces a single thickness of fabric and is usually used where a colour is only required in a particular area of a row and does not form a repeating pattern across the row, as in the fairisle technique.

Intarsia: The simplest way to do this is to cut short lengths of yarn for each motif or block of colour used in a row. Then joining in the various colours at the appropriate point on the row, link one colour to the next by twisting them around each other where they meet on the wrong side to avoid gaps. All ends can then either be darned along the colour join lines, as each motif is completed or then can be "knitted-in" to the fabric of the knitting as each colour is worked into the pattern. This is done in much the same way as "weaving-in" yarns when working the Fairisle technique and does save time darning-in ends. It is essential that the tension is noted for Intarsia as this may vary from the stocking stitch if both are used in the same pattern.

Finishing Instructions

After working for hours knitting a garment, it seems a great pity that many garments are spoiled because such little care is taken in the pressing and finishing process. Follow the following tips for a truly professional-looking garment.

Pressing

Block out each piece of knitting and following the instructions on the ball band press the garment pieces, omitting the ribs. Tip: Take special care to press the edges, as this will make sewing up both easier and neater. If the ball band indicates that the fabric is not to be pressed, then covering the blocked out fabric with a damp white cotton cloth and leaving it to stand will have the desired effect. Darn in all ends neatly along the selvedge edge or a colour join, as appropriate.

Stitching

When stitching the pieces together, remember to match areas of colour and texture very carefully where they meet. Use a seam stitch such as back stitch or mattress stitch for all main knitting seams and join all ribs and neckband with mattress stitch, unless otherwise stated.

Construction

Having completed the pattern instructions, join left shoulder and neckband seams as detailed above. Sew the top of the sleeve to the body of the garment using the method detailed in the pattern, referring to the appropriate guide:

Set-in sleeves: Place centre of cast-off edge of sleeve to shoulder seam. Set in sleeve, easing sleeve head into armhole.
Straight cast-off sleeves: Place centre of cast-off edge of sleeve to shoulder seam. Sew top of sleeve to body.
Shallow set-in sleeves. Place centre of cast off edge of sleeve to shoulder seam. Match decreases at beg of armhole shaping to decreases at top of sleeve. Sew sleeve head into armhole, easing in shapings. Join side and sleeve seams.
Slip stitch pocket edgings and linings into place. Sew on buttons to correspond with buttonholes. Ribbed welts and neckbands and any area of garter stitch should not be pressed.

Abbreviations

K	knit	psso	pass slipped stitch over
P	purl		
st(s)	stitch(es)	tbl	through back of loop
inc	increas(e)(ing)		
dec	decreas(e)(ing)	M1	make one stitch by picking up horizontal loop before next stitch and working into back of it
st st	stocking stitch (1 row K, 1 row P)		
g st	garter stitch (K every row)		
beg	begin(ning)		
foll	following	yrn	yarn round needle
rem	remain(ing)	yfwd	yarn forward
rep	repeat	yon	yarn over needle
alt	alternate	yfrn	yarn forward and round needle
cont	continue		
patt	pattern	meas	measures
tog	together	o	no stitches, times, or rows
mm	millimetres		
cm	centimetres	-	no stitches, times or rows for that size
in(s)	inch(es)		
RS	right side		
WS	wrong side	approx	approximately
sl 1	slip one stitch	rev	reverse
sl 2	slip two stitches		

Main image page 12

 Alphabet Blanket

YARN

RYC Cashsoft DK

A	Tape	515	4	x 50gm
B	Kingfisher	525	1	x 50gm
C	Cashew	522	1	x 50gm
D	Bloom	520	1	x 50gm
E	Donkey	517	1	x 50gm
F	Lichen	523	1	x 50gm
G	Navy	514	1	x 50gm

NEEDLES

1 pair 4mm (no 8) (US 6) needles
Cable needle

TENSION

23½ sts and 30 rows to 10 cm measured over
pattern using 4mm (US 6) needles.

FINISHED SIZE

Completed blanket measures 52 cm (20½ in) wide
and 60 cm (23½ in) long, including edging.

SPECIAL ABBREVIATIONS

C8B = slip next 4 sts onto cable needle and
leave at back of work, K4, then K4 from cable
needle.

CENTRE SECTION

Using 4mm (US 6) needles and yarn A cast on
109 sts.
Using the **intarsia** technique as described on the
information page, work in patt from chart until all
163 rows have been completed, ending with **WS**
facing for next row.
Cast off in patt (on **WS**).

MAKING UP

Press as described on the information page.
Edging
Using 4mm (US 6) needles and yarn A cast on 10 sts.
Row 1 (RS): P2, K8.
Row 2: K2, P8.
Rows 3 to 6: As rows 1 and 2, twice.
Row 7: P2, C8B.
Row 8: As row 2.
Rows 9 and 10: As rows 1 and 2.
These 10 rows form patt.
Cont in patt until edging, unstretched, fits around
entire outer edge of centre section, easing it
around the corners so that it lays flat and ending
with RS facing for next row.
Cast off in patt.
Join cast-on and cast-off ends of edging, then
slip st edging in place.

Key

□ A - K on RS,
  P on WS

▣ P on RS,
  K on WS

▱ C8B

▣ B ⎤
□ C ⎮
□ D ⎰ K on RS,
▣ E ⎱ P on WS
▣ F ⎮
▣ G ⎦

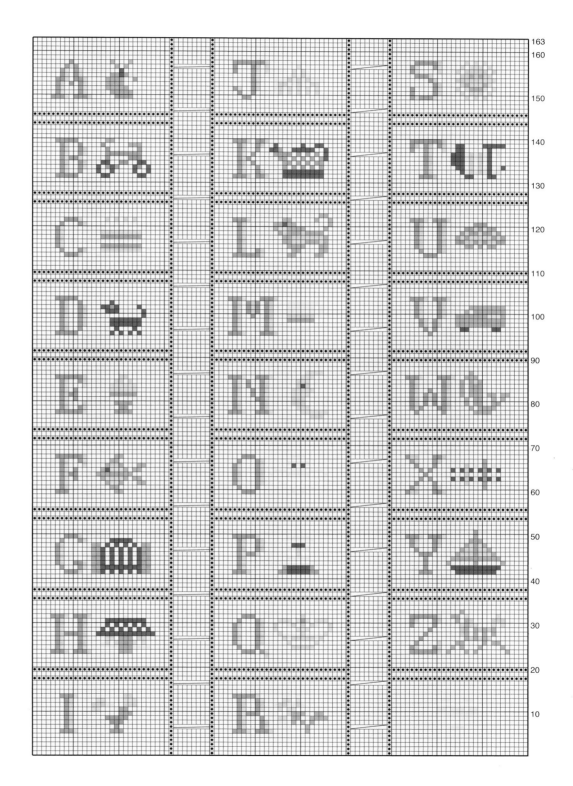

Main image page 16

 Angelica

YARN

	S	M	L	XL	
To fit bust	81-86	91-97	102-107	112-117	cm
	32-34	36-38	40-42	44-46	in

RYC Cashsoft DK

	9	10	11	12	x 50gm

(photographed in Bloom 520)

NEEDLES

1 pair 3¼mm (no 10) (US 3) needles
1 pair 4mm (no 8) (US 6) needles
Cable needle
2 double-pointed 3¼mm (no 10) (US 3) needles
1 yarn holder

TENSION

27 sts and 30 rows to 10 cm measured over rib when slightly stretched using 4mm (US 6) needles.

SPECIAL ABBREVIATIONS

C8B = slip next 4 sts onto cable needle and leave at back of work, K4, then K4 from cable needle.

BACK

Using 4mm (US 6) needles cast on 111 [125: 141: 157] sts.
Row 1 (RS): K0 [0: 0: 2], P0 [1: 3: 3], *K3, P3, rep from * to last 3 [4: 0: 2] sts, K3 [3: 0: 2], P0 [1: 0: 0].
Row 2: P0 [0: 0: 2], K0 [1: 3: 3], *P3, K3, rep from * to last 3 [4: 0: 2] sts, P3 [3: 0: 2], K0 [1: 0: 0].
These 2 rows form rib.
Cont in rib, shaping side seams by inc 1 st at each end of 5th and 2 foll 6th rows, then on 4 foll 8th rows, taking inc sts into rib. 125 [139: 155: 171] sts.
Work 7 [9: 13: 15] rows, ending with RS facing for next row. (Back should meas 19 [20: 21: 22] cm.)
Shape armholes
Keeping rib correct, cast off 8 [9: 10: 11] sts at beg of next 2 rows. 109 [121: 135: 149] sts.
Dec 1 st at each end of next 5 [7: 9: 11] rows, then on foll 3 [4: 5: 6] alt rows, then on 2 foll 4th rows. 89 [95: 103: 111] sts.
Cont straight until armhole meas 20 [21: 22: 23] cm, ending with RS facing for next row.
Shape shoulders and back neck
Cast off 8 [9: 10: 11] sts at beg of next 2 rows. 73 [77: 83: 89] sts.

Next row (RS): Cast off 8 [9: 10: 11] sts, rib until there are 12 [13: 14: 16] sts on right needle and turn, leaving rem sts on a holder.
Work each side of neck separately.
Cast off 4 sts at beg of next row.
Cast off rem 8 [9: 10: 12] sts.
With RS facing, rejoin yarn to rem sts, cast off centre 33 [33: 35: 35] sts, rib to end.
Complete to match first side, reversing shapings.

LEFT FRONT

Using 4mm (US 6) needles cast on 56 [63: 71: 79] sts.
Row 1 (RS): K0 [0: 0: 2], P0 [1: 3: 3], *K3, P3, rep from * to last 2 sts, K2.
Row 2: P2, K3, *P3, K3, rep from * to last 3 [4: 0: 2] sts, P3 [3: 0: 2], K0 [1: 0: 0].
These 2 rows form rib.
Work 2 rows, ending with RS facing for next row.
Shape front slope
Keeping rib correct, dec 1 st at end of next and 7 [4: 4: 1] foll 4th rows, then on 4 [6: 7: 9] foll 6th rows **and at same time** inc 1 st at beg of 3rd and 2 foll 6th rows, then on 4 foll 8th rows, taking inc sts into rib.
51 [59: 66: 75] sts.
Work 1 [3: 1: 3] rows, ending with RS facing for next row. (Left front should match back to beg of armhole shaping.)
Shape armhole
Cast off 8 [9: 10: 11] sts at beg of next row.
43 [50: 56: 64] sts.
Work 1 row.
Dec 1 st at armhole edge of next 5 [7: 9: 11] rows, then on foll 3 [4: 5: 6] alt rows, then on 2 foll 4th rows **and at same time** dec 1 st at front slope edge of 3rd [next: 3rd: next] and every foll 6th row. 30 [33: 35: 39] sts.
Dec 1 st at front slope edge **only** on 2nd [2nd: 6th: 6th] and every foll 6th row until 24 [27: 30: 34] sts rem.
Cont straight until left front matches back to beg of shoulder shaping, ending with RS facing for next row.
Shape shoulder
Cast off 8 [9: 10: 11] sts at beg of next and foll alt row.

Work 1 row.
Cast off rem 8 [9: 10: 12] sts.

RIGHT FRONT

Using 4mm (US 6) needles cast on 56 [63: 71: 79] sts.
Row 1 (RS): K2, P3, *K3, P3, rep from * to last 3 [4: 0: 2] sts, K3 [3: 0: 2], P0 [1: 0: 0].
Row 2: P0 [0: 0: 2], K0 [1: 3: 3], *P3, K3, rep from * to last 2 sts, P2.
These 2 rows form rib.
Work 2 rows, ending with RS facing for next row.
Shape front slope
Keeping rib correct, dec 1 st at beg of next and 7 [4: 4: 1] foll 4th rows, then on 4 [6: 7: 9] foll 6th rows **and at same time** inc 1 st at end of 3rd and 2 foll 6th rows, then on 4 foll 8th rows, taking inc sts into rib.
51 [59: 66: 75] sts.
Complete to match left front, reversing shapings.

SLEEVES

Using 3¼mm (US 3) needles cast on 63 [65: 67: 67] sts.
Row 1 (RS): P0 [1: 2: 2], *K3, P3, rep from * to last 3 [4: 5: 5] sts, K3, P0 [1: 2: 2].
Row 2: K0 [1: 2: 2], *P3, K3, rep from * to last 3 [4: 5: 5] sts, P3, K0 [1: 2: 2].
These 2 rows form rib.
Work in rib for a further 6 rows, ending with RS facing for next row.
Change to 4mm (US 6) needles.
Cont in rib, shaping sides by inc 1 st at each end of next and every foll 8th [8th: 8th: 6th] row to 69 [79: 87: 75] sts, then on every foll 10th [10th: 10th: 8th] row until there are 89 [93: 97: 101] sts, taking inc sts into rib.
Cont straight until sleeve meas 46 [47: 48: 48] cm, ending with RS facing for next row.
Shape top
Cast off 8 [9: 10: 11] sts at beg of next 2 rows.
73 [75: 77: 79] sts.
Dec 1 st at each end of next 5 rows, then on foll 3 alt rows, then on every foll 4th row until 49 [51: 53: 55] sts rem.
Work 1 row.
Dec 1 st at each end of next and every foll alt row

until 37 sts rem, then on foll 5 rows, ending with RS facing for next row.
Cast off rem 27 sts.

MAKING UP

Press as described on the information page.
Join both shoulder seams using back stitch, or mattress stitch if preferred. Join side seams.

Hem border

Using 3¼mm (US 3) needles cast on 20 sts.
Row 1 (WS): sl 1, (K2, yfwd, K2tog) twice, K5, K2tog, yfwd, K3, inc in last st. 21 sts.
Row 2: K6, yfwd, sl 1, K1, psso, K3, K2tog, yfwd, K4, yfwd, K2tog, K2.
Row 3: sl 1, K2, yfwd, K2tog, K4, yfwd, sl 1, K1, psso, K1, K2tog, yfwd, K6, inc in last st. 22 sts.
Row 4: K9, yfwd, sl 1, K2tog, psso, yfwd, K6, yfwd, K2tog, K2.
Row 5: sl 1, K2, yfwd, K2tog, K4, K2tog, yfwd, K1, yfwd, K2tog, K4, (yfwd) twice, K3, inc in last st. 25 sts.
Row 6: K5, (K1, P1) into double yfwd of previous row, K3, K2tog, yfwd, K3, yfwd, sl 1, K1, psso, K4, yfwd, K2tog, K2.
Row 7: sl 1, K2, yfwd, K2tog, K2, K2tog, yfwd, K5, yfwd, sl 1, K1, psso, K9.
Row 8: Cast off 5 sts (one st on right needle after cast-off), K2, K2tog, yfwd, K7, yfwd, sl 1, K1, psso, K2, yfwd, K2tog, K2. 20 sts.
These 8 rows form patt.
Cont in patt until straight edge of hem border, unstretched, fits around entire front and back cast-on edges, ending after patt row 8.
Cast off.
Slip st border in place.

Front trim

Using 4mm (US 6) needles cast on 10 sts.
Row 1 (RS): P2, K8.
Row 2: P8, K2.
Rows 3 and 4: As rows 1 and 2.
Row 5: P2, C8B.
Row 6: As row 2.
Rows 7 to 10: As rows 1 and 2, twice.
These 10 rows form patt.
Cont in patt until front trim, when slightly stretched, fits up entire right front opening edge, across back neck and down entire left front opening edge, ending after patt row 6.
Cast off.
Slip st trim in place.
See information page for finishing instructions, setting in sleeves using the set-in method.

Ties (make 2)

Using double-pointed 3¼mm (US 3) needles cast on 3 sts.
Row 1 (RS): K3, *without turning slip these 3 sts to opposite end of needle and bring yarn to opposite end of work pulling it quite tightly across **WS** of work, K these 3 sts again, rep from * until tie is 26 cm long, K3tog and fasten off.
Attach ties to front opening edges level with top of hem border.

46.5 [51.5: 57.5: 63.5] cm
(18½ [20½: 22½: 25] in)

48 [50: 52: 54] cm
(19 [19½: 20½: 21½] in)

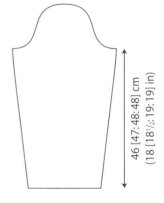

46 [47: 48: 48] cm
(18 [18½: 19: 19] in)

Main image page 24

YARN

	1-2	2-3	3-4	4-5	years
To fit chest	56	58	61	64	cm
	22	23	24	25	in

RYC Cashsoft DK

	5	6	6	7	x 50gm

(photographed in Bella Donna 502)

NEEDLES

1 pair 3¼mm (no 10) (US 3) needles
1 pair 4mm (no 8) (US 6) needles
3¼mm (no 10) (US 3) circular needle
1 yarn holder

RIBBON – approx 2 m of narrow satin ribbon

TENSION

22 sts and 30 rows to 10 cm measured over pattern using 4mm (US 6) needles.

SPECIAL ABBREVIATION

wrap3 = yfwd, K3, lift 3rd st on right needle over first and 2nd sts and off right needle.

BACK

Using 3¼mm (US 3) needles cast on 58 [62: 64: 68] sts.

Rows 1 to 3: Knit.
Row 4 (eyelet row) (WS): P1, *yrn, P2tog, rep from * to last st, P1.
Rows 5 and 6: Knit.
Place markers at both ends of last row.
Change to 4mm (US 6) needles.
Beg and ending rows as indicated and repeating the 16 row patt repeat throughout, cont in patt from chart as folls:
Work 2 rows, ending with RS facing for next row.
Inc 1 st at each end of next and every foll 6th [6th: 8th: 8th] row until there are 68 [72: 74: 78] sts, taking inc sts into patt.
Cont straight until back meas 13 [14: 16: 17] cm, ending with RS facing for next row.
Shape armholes
Keeping patt correct, cast off 4 sts at beg of next 2 rows. 60 [64: 66: 70] sts.
Dec 1 st at each end of next 3 rows, then on foll 2 [3: 3: 4] alt rows. 50 [52: 54: 56] sts.
Cont straight until armhole meas 12 [13: 13: 14] cm, ending with RS facing for next row.
Shape shoulders and back neck
Next row (RS): Cast off 7 [7: 7: 8] sts, patt until there are 8 [9: 9: 9] sts on right needle and turn, leaving rem sts on a holder.
Work each side of neck separately.

Dec 1 st at beg of next row.
Cast off rem 7 [8: 8: 8] sts.
With RS facing, rejoin yarn to rem sts, cast off centre 20 [20: 22: 22] sts, patt to end.
Complete to match first side, reversing shapings.

LEFT FRONT

Using 4mm (US 6) needles cast on 12 [14: 15: 17] sts.
Beg and ending rows as indicated, cont in patt from chart as folls:
Work 1 row, ending with **WS** facing for next row.
Shape front opening edge
Cast on 4 sts at beg of next and foll alt row **and at same time** inc 1 st at beg of 2nd row, taking inc sts into patt. 21 [23: 24: 26] sts.
Work 1 row, ending with **WS** facing for next row.
Inc 1 st at front opening edge of next 4 rows, then on foll 5 alt rows **and at same time** inc 1 st at side seam edge of 4th [4th: 6th: 6th] and foll 6th [6th: 8th: 8th] row. 32 [34: 35: 37] sts.
Inc 1 st at side seam edge **only** on 2nd [2nd: 8th: 8th] and every foll 6th [6th: 8th: 8th] row until there are 34 [36: 37: 39] sts.
Cont straight until left front matches back to beg of armhole shaping, **measuring back from markers not cast-on edge**, ending with RS facing

Key

□ K on RS,
P on WS

◙ yfwd

◩ sl 1, K1, psso

▱ wrap 3

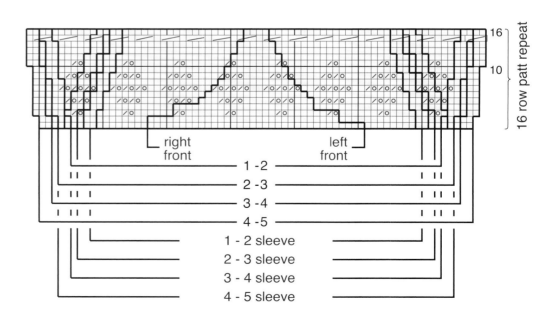

16 row patt repeat

right front   left front

1 - 2
2 - 3
3 - 4
4 - 5

1 - 2 sleeve
2 - 3 sleeve
3 - 4 sleeve
4 - 5 sleeve

for next row.

Shape armhole and front slope

Keeping patt correct, cast off 4 sts at beg and dec 1 st at end of next row.
29 [31: 32: 34] sts.
Work 1 row.
Dec 1 st at armhole edge of next 3 rows, then on foll 2 [3: 3: 4] alt rows **and at same time** dec 1 st at front slope edge of next and foll 3 [3: 4: 4] alt rows. 20 [21: 21: 22] sts.
Dec 1 st at front slope edge **only** on 2nd and foll 1 [0: 0: 0] alt row, then on every foll 4th row until 14 [15: 15: 16] sts rem.
Cont straight until left front matches back to beg of shoulder shaping, ending with RS facing for next row.

Shape shoulder

Cast off 7 [7: 7: 8] sts at beg of next row.
Work 1 row.
Cast off rem 7 [8: 8: 8] sts.

RIGHT FRONT

Using 4mm (US 6) needles cast on 12 [14: 15: 17] sts.
Beg and ending rows as indicated, cont in patt from chart as foll:
Work 2 rows, ending with RS facing for next row.

Shape front opening edge

Cast on 4 sts at beg of next and foll alt row **and at same time** inc 1 st at end of next row, taking inc sts into patt. 21 [23: 24: 26] sts.
Complete to match left front, reversing shapings.

SLEEVES

Using 3¼mm (US 3) needles cast on 52 [56: 58: 62] sts.
Rows 1 to 3: Knit.
Row 4 (eyelet row) (WS): P1, *yrn, P2tog, rep from * to last st, P1.
Rows 5 and 6: Knit.
Change to 4mm (US 6) needles.
Beg and ending rows as indicated, cont in patt from chart, shaping sides by dec 1 st at each end of next and 4 [4: 6: 6] foll 3rd rows, then on 2 [3: 2: 3] foll 4th rows. 38 [40: 40: 42] sts.
Work 7 rows, ending with RS facing for next row.
Inc 1 st at each end of next and every foll 4th [4th: 6th: 6th] row to 44 [44: 48: 46] sts, then

on every foll 6th [6th: -: 8th] row until there are 46 [48: -: 50] sts, taking inc sts into patt.
Cont straight until sleeve meas 20 [22: 24: 27] cm, ending with RS facing for next row.

Shape top

Keeping patt correct, cast off 4 sts at beg of next 2 rows. 38 [40: 40: 42] sts.
Dec 1 st at each end of next 3 rows, then on foll 3 alt rows, then on every foll 4th row until 20 [22: 22: 24] sts rem.
Work 1 row.
Dec 1 st at each end of next and every foll 0 [1: 1: 2] alt rows, then on foll row, ending with RS facing for next row.
Cast off rem 16 sts.

MAKING UP

Press as described on the information page.
Join both shoulder seams using back stitch, or mattress stitch if preferred.

Front band

With RS facing and using 3¼mm (US 3) circular needle, beg and ending at side seams, pick up and knit 12 [14: 15: 17] sts from right front cast-on edge, 22 sts up shaped row-end edge to last inc, 9 [13: 18: 20] sts up straight row-end edge to beg of front slope shaping, 29 [30: 30: 32] sts up right front slope, 22 [22: 24: 24] sts from back, 29 [30: 30: 32] sts down left front slope to beg of front slope shaping, 9 [13: 18: 20] sts down straight row-end edge to last inc, 22 sts down shaped row-end edge to cast-on edge, then 12 [14:

15: 17] sts from left front cast-on edge.
166 [180: 194: 206] sts.
Rows 1 and 2: Knit.
Row 3 (eyelet row) (WS): P1, *yrn, P2tog, rep from * to last st, P1.
Rows 4 to 6: Knit.
Cast off knitwise (on **WS**).
See information page for finishing instructions, setting in sleeves using the set-in method and matching cast-off edge of front band to cast-on edge of back.

Edging

Using 3¼mm (US 3) needles cast on 3 sts.
Row 1 (WS): P3.
Row 2: K1, yfwd, K1 tbl, P1. 4 sts.
Row 3: P2, (K1, P1, K1, P1) all into yfwd of previous row, P1. 7 sts.
Row 4: Cast off 4 sts (one st on right needle after cast-off), K1 tbl, P1. 3 sts.
These 4 rows form patt.
Cont in patt until edging fits around entire lower edge, front opening and back neck edges of body, ending after patt row 4 and with **WS** facing for next row.
Cast off (on **WS**).
Join cast-on and cast-off ends of edging, then slip st edging in place.
Work edging around lower edge of sleeves in same way.
Using photograph as a guide, thread ribbon through eyelet rows of back, front band and sleeves.

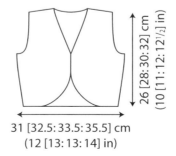

31 [32.5: 33.5: 35.5] cm
(12 [13: 13: 14] in)

26 [28: 30: 32] cm
(10 [11: 12: 12½] in)

20 [22: 24: 27] cm
(8 [8½: 9½: 10½] in)

Main image page 10

YARN

	0-3	3-6	6-12	12-18	months
To fit chest	41	46	51	56	cm
	16	18	20	22	in

RYC Cashsoft DK

	2	2	3	4	x 50gm

Small amounts of same yarn in 3 contrast colours for embroidery
(photographed in Sweet 501, embroidered with Bloom 520, Lime 509 and Mirage 503)

NEEDLES

1 pair 3¼mm (no 10) (US 3) needles
1 pair 4mm (no 8) (US 6) needles
1 yarn holder

BUTTONS – 6 x 00333

TENSION

22 sts and 30 rows to 10 cm measured over stocking stitch using 4mm (US 6) needles.

SPECIAL ABBREVIATIONS

MB = (K1, P1, K1) all into next st, turn, P3, turn, K3, turn, P3, turn, sl 1, K2tog, psso.

LEFT FRONT

Using 3¼mm (US 3) needles cast on 30 [33: 36: 39] sts.
Row 1 (RS): K0 [1: 0: 1], *P1, K1, rep from * to end.
Row 2: *P1, K1, rep from * to last 0 [1: 0: 1] st, P0 [1: 0: 1].
These 2 rows form rib.
Cont in rib for a further 11 rows, ending with **WS** facing for next row.
Row 14 (WS): Rib 5 and slip these sts onto a holder, rib to end. 25 [28: 31: 34] sts.
Change to 4mm (US 6) needles.
Place chart
Row 1 (RS): Inc in first st, K to last 16 sts, work last 16 sts as row 1 of chart for left front.
Row 2: Work first 16 sts as row 2 of chart for left front, P to last 1 [0: 0: 0] st, (inc in last st) 1 [0: 0: 0] times. 27 [29: 32: 35] sts.
These 2 rows set the sts – front opening edge

16 sts worked foll chart and rem sts in st st.
Keeping sts correct as set, inc 1 st at beg of next and foll 0 [6: 8: 13] alt rows, then at same edge on foll 3 [0: 7: 7] rows. 31 [36: 48: 56] sts.
Work 0 [1: 0: 0] row, ending with RS facing for next row.
Cast on 3 [4: 4: 5] sts at beg of next and foll 3 alt rows. 43 [52: 64: 76] sts.
Work 12 [14: 14: 16] rows, ending with **WS** facing for next row.
Shape neck
Keeping patt correct, cast off 7 [8: 8: 9] sts at beg of next row. 36 [44: 56: 67] sts.
Dec 1 st at neck edge of next 3 rows, then on foll 1 [1: 2: 2] alt rows. 32 [40: 51: 62] sts.
Work 1 row.
Inc 1 st at neck edge of next row, ending with **WS** facing for next row.
33 [41: 52: 63] sts.
Break yarn and leave sts on a holder.

RIGHT FRONT

Using 3¼mm (US 3) needles cast on 30 [33: 36: 39] sts.
Row 1 (RS): *K1, P1, rep from * to last 0 [1: 0: 1] st, K0 [1: 0: 1].
Row 2: P0 [1: 0: 1], *K1, P1, rep from * to end.
These 2 rows form rib.
Cont in rib for a further 2 rows, ending with RS

facing for next row.
Row 5 (RS): K1, P2tog, yrn (to make first buttonhole), rib to end.
Work in rib for a further 8 rows, ending with **WS** facing for next row.
Row 14 (WS): Rib to last 5 sts and turn, leaving rem 5 sts on a holder. 25 [28: 31: 34] sts.
Change to 4mm (US 6) needles.
Place chart
Row 1 (RS): Work first 16 sts as row 1 of chart for right front, K to last st, inc in last st.
Row 2: (Inc in first st) 1 [0: 0: 0] times, P to last 16 sts, work last 16 sts as row 2 of chart for right front. 27 [29: 32: 35] sts.
These 2 rows set the sts – front opening edge 16 sts worked foll chart and rem sts in st st.
Keeping sts correct as set, inc 1 st at end of next and foll 0 [6: 8: 13] alt rows, then at same edge on foll 3 [0: 7: 7] rows. 31 [36: 48: 56] sts.
Complete to match left front, reversing shapings, but do NOT break yarn.

BACK (worked downwards)

Using 4mm (US 6) needles and with **WS** facing, P across 33 [41: 52: 63] sts of right front, turn and cast on 19 [21: 23: 25] sts, turn and P across 33 [41: 52: 63] sts on left front.
85 [103: 127: 151] sts.
Beg with a K row, work in st st for 17 [19: 21: 23]

Right front   Left front

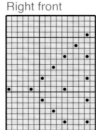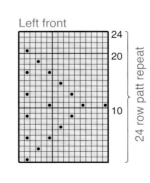

24 row patt repeat

Key
☐ K on RS,
P on WS

▣ MB

rows, ending with **WS** facing for next row.

Shape for sleeves

Cast off 3 [4: 4: 5] sts at beg of next 8 rows, ending with **WS** facing for next row.
61 [71: 95: 111] sts.
Work 0 [1: 0: 0] row.
Dec 1 st at each end of next 5 [1: 8: 8] rows, then on foll 0 [6: 8: 13] alt rows.
51 [57: 63: 69] sts.
Work 0 [1: 1: 1] row, ending with RS facing for next row.
Change to 3¼mm (US 3) needles.
Next row (RS): Work 2 tog, K1 [0: 1: 0], *P1, K1, rep from * to last 2 [3: 2: 3] sts, P0 [1: 0: 1], work 2 tog. 49 [55: 61: 67] sts.
Next row: K1 [0: 1: 0], *P1, K1, rep from * to last 0 [1: 0: 1] st, P0 [1: 0: 1].
This row sets position of rib.
Work in rib for a further 12 rows, ending with RS facing for next row.
Cast off in rib.

MAKING UP

Press as described on the information page.

Button band

Slip 5 sts from left front holder onto 3¼mm (US 3) needles and rejoin yarn with RS facing.

Cont in rib as set until button band, when slightly stretched, fits up left front opening edge to neck shaping, ending with RS facing for next row.
Break yarn and leave sts on a holder.
Slip stitch band in place.
Mark positions for 6 buttons on this band – first to come level with buttonhole already worked in right front, last to come just above neck shaping, and rem 4 buttons evenly spaced between.

Buttonhole band

Slip 5 sts from right front holder onto 3¼mm (US 3) needles and rejoin yarn with **WS** facing.
Cont in rib as set until buttonhole band, when slightly stretched, fits up right front opening edge to neck shaping, ending with RS facing for next row and with the addition of a further 4 buttonholes worked to correspond with positions marked for buttons as folls:
Buttonhole row (RS): K1, P2tog, yrn (to make a buttonhole), P1, K1.
When band is complete, do NOT break yarn.
Slip stitch band in place.

Neckband

With RS facing and using 3¼mm (US 3) needles, rib 5 sts of buttonhole band, pick up and knit 13 [14: 16: 17] sts up right side of neck, 19 [21: 23: 25] sts from back, and 13 [14: 16: 17] sts down

left side of neck, then rib 5 sts of button band.
55 [59: 65: 69] sts.
Work in rib as set by bands for 1 row, ending with RS facing for next row.
Row 2 (RS): K1, P2tog, yrn (to make 6th buttonhole), rib to end.
Work in rib for a further 2 rows, ending with **WS** facing for next row.
Cast off in rib (on **WS**).

Cuffs (both alike)

With RS facing and using 3¼mm (US 3) needles, pick up and knit 31 [33: 35: 37] sts evenly along straight row-end edge of back and fronts.
Row 1 (WS): P1, *K1, P1, rep from * to end.
Row 2: K1, *P1, K1, rep from * to end.
These 2 rows form rib.
Work in rib for a further 11 rows, ending with RS facing for next row.
Cast off in rib.
See information page for finishing instructions.
Using photograph as a guide, work embroidery on fronts as folls: work 3 cross stitches around bobble inside triangles, working each stitch in a different colour. Embroider flowers between triangles by working 5 or 6 lazy daisy stitches radiating out from one point, and a french knot at centre.

Lazy Daisy

French Knot

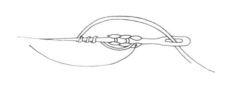

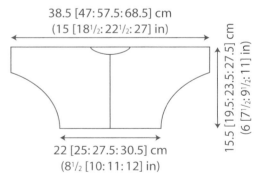

38.5 [47: 57.5: 68.5] cm
(15 [18½: 22½: 27] in)

15.5 [19.5: 23.5: 27.5] cm
(6 [7½: 9½: 11] in)

22 [25: 27.5: 30.5] cm
(8½ [10: 11: 12] in)

Main image page 34

 Butterscotch

YARN

	1-2	2-3	3-4	4-5	years
To fit chest	56	58	61	64	cm
	22	23	24	25	in

RYC Natural Silk Aran

	7	8	9	10	x 50gm

(photographed in Palm Leaf 462)

NEEDLES

1 pair 4mm (no 8) (US 6) needles
1 pair 4½mm (no 7) (US 7) needles
1 yarn holder

BUTTONS – 2 x 00408

TENSION

18 sts and 30 rows to 10 cm measured over moss stitch using 4½mm (US 7) needles.

BACK

Using 4mm (US 6) needles cast on 58 [62: 66: 66] sts.
Row 1 (RS): K2, *P2, K2, rep from * to end.
Row 2: P2, *K2, P2, rep from * to end.
These 2 rows form rib.
Cont in rib for a further 5 rows, ending with **WS** facing for next row.
Row 8 (WS): Rib 9 [6: 6: 10], work 2 tog, (rib 17 [10: 11: 20], work 2 tog) 2 [4: 4: 2] times, rib to end.
55 [57: 61: 63] sts.
Change to 4½mm (US 7) needles.
Row 1 (RS): K1, *P1, K1, rep from * to end.
Row 2: As row 1.
These 2 rows form moss st.
Cont in moss st until back meas 16 [17: 19: 20] cm, ending with RS facing for next row.
Shape raglan armholes
Cast off 2 sts at beg of next 2 rows.
51 [53: 57: 59] sts.
Dec 1 st at each end of next and 4 [4: 3: 3] foll 4th rows, then on every foll alt row until 17 [17: 19: 19] sts rem.

Work 1 row, ending with RS facing for next row. Cast off in moss st.

FRONT

Work as given for back until 43 [43: 47: 47] sts rem in raglan armhole shaping.
Work 3 [1: 1: 1] rows, ending with RS facing for next row.
Divide for front opening
Next row (RS): Work 2 tog, moss st 17 [17: 19: 19] sts and turn, leaving rem sts on a holder.
Work each side of neck separately.
Dec 1 st at raglan armhole edge of 2nd and foll 7 alt rows, ending with **WS** facing for next row. 10 [10: 12: 12] sts.
Shape neck
Cast off 5 sts at beg of next row. 5 [5: 7: 7] sts.
Dec 1 st at neck edge of next 2 rows, then on foll 0 [0: 1: 1] alt row **and at same time** dec 1 st at raglan armhole edge of next and foll 0 [0: 1: 1] alt row, ending with RS facing for next row. 2 sts.
Next row (RS): K2tog and fasten off.
With RS facing, rejoin yarn to rem sts, cast off centre 5 sts, moss st to last 2 sts, work 2 tog.
Complete to match first side, reversing shapings.

SLEEVES

Using 4mm (US 6) needles cast on 34 [38: 38: 38] sts.
Work in rib as given for back for 7 rows, ending with **WS** facing for next row.
Row 8 (WS): Rib 5 [2: 2: 5], work 2 tog, (rib 9 [6: 6: 11], work 2 tog) 2 [4: 4: 2] times, rib to end.
31 [33: 33: 35] sts.
Change to 4½mm (US 7) needles.
Work in moss st as given for back, shaping sides by inc 1 st at each end of 3rd and every foll 4th row to 51 [53: 51: 49] sts, then on every foll - [6th: 6th: 6th] row until there are - [55: 55: 59] sts.
Cont straight until sleeve meas 20 [22: 24: 27] cm, ending with RS facing for next row.
Shape raglan
Cast off 2 sts at beg of next 2 rows.

47 [51: 51: 55] sts.
Dec 1 st at each end of next and 4 [3: 3: 2] foll 4th rows, then on every foll alt row until 19 sts rem.
Work 1 row, ending with RS facing for next row.
Left sleeve only
Dec 1 st at each end of next row, then cast off 4 sts at beg of foll row. 13 sts.
Dec 1 st at beg of next row, then cast off 4 sts at beg of foll row. 8 sts.
Right sleeve only
Cast off 5 sts at beg and dec 1 st at end of next row. 13 sts.
Work 1 row.
Cast off 4 sts at beg and dec 1 st at end of next row. 8 sts.
Work 1 row.
Both sleeves
Rep last 2 rows once more.
Cast off rem 3 sts.

MAKING UP

Press as described on the information page.
Join raglan seams using back stitch, or mattress stitch if preferred.
Button band
With RS facing and using 4mm (US 6) needles, pick up and knit 12 sts evenly along one front opening edge (left front for a girl, or right front for a boy), between neck shaping and base of opening.
Row 1 (WS): K1, *P2, K2, rep from * to last 3 sts, P2, K1.
Row 2: K3, *P2, K2, rep from * to last st, K1.
These 2 rows form rib.
Work in rib for a further 4 rows, ending with **WS** facing for next row.
Cast off in rib (on **WS**).
Buttonhole band
Work to match button band, picking up sts along other front opening edge and with the addition of 2 buttonholes in row 4 worked as folls:
Row 4 (RS): Rib 1, work 2 tog, yrn, rib 6, work 2 tog, yrn, rib 1.

Lay buttonhole band over button band and sew row-end edges to cast-off sts at base of opening.

Collar

With RS facing and using 4mm (US 6) needles, beg and ending halfway across top of bands, pick up and knit 9 [9: 10: 12] sts up right side of neck, 10 sts from right sleeve, 18 [18: 20: 20] sts from back, 10 sts from left sleeve, then 9 [9: 10: 12] sts down left side of neck. 56 [56: 60: 64] sts.

Beg with row 2, work in rib as given for button band for 13 rows, ending with **WS** of collar (RS of body) facing for next row.

Next row (WS of collar): K1, *P2, K1, M1, K1, rep from * to last 3 sts, P2, K1. 69 [69: 74: 79] sts.

Next row: K3, *P3, K2, rep from * to last st, K1.

Next row: K1, *P2, K3, rep from * to last 3 sts, P2, K1.

Rep last 2 rows until collar meas 9 cm from pick-up row, ending with RS facing for next row.

Cast off in rib.

See information page for finishing instructions.

30.5 [31.5: 34: 35] cm
(12 [12½: 13½: 14] in)

30 [32: 34: 36] cm
(12 [12½: 13½: 14] in)

20 [22: 24: 27] cm
(8 [8½: 9½: 10½] in)

 Hazel

YARN

	S	M	L	XL	
To fit bust	81-86	91-97	102-107	112-117	cm
	32-34	36-38	40-42	44-46	in

RYC Natural Silk Aran

	19	21	23	25	x 50gm

(photographed in Palm Leaf 462)

NEEDLES

1 pair 4mm (no 8) (US 6) needles
1 pair 4½mm (no 7) (US 7) needles
Cable needle

EXTRAS – 1 decorative kilt pin x 00412

TENSION

18 sts and 34 rows to 10 cm measured over garter stitch using 4½mm (US 7) needles.

SPECIAL ABBREVIATIONS

C4B = slip next 2 sts onto cable needle and leave at back of work, K2, then K2 from cable needle.

BACK

Using 4mm (US 6) needles cast on 86 [96: 106: 116] sts.
Beg with a K row, work in st st for 5 rows, ending with **WS** facing for next row.
Change to 4½mm (US 7) needles.
Work in g st until back meas 27 [28: 29: 30] cm **allowing first few rows to roll to RS**, ending with RS facing for next row.

Shape raglan armholes

Cast off 3 sts at beg of next 2 rows.
80 [90: 100: 110] sts.
Dec 1 st at each end of next and foll 13 [21: 27: 36] alt rows, then on every foll 4th row until 24 [24: 26: 26] sts rem.
Work 3 rows, ending with RS facing for next row.
Cast off.

LEFT FRONT

Using 4mm (US 6) needles cast on 54 [59: 64: 69] sts.

Beg with a K row, work in st st for 5 rows, ending with **WS** facing for next row.
Change to 4½mm (US 7) needles.
Work in g st until left front matches back to beg of raglan armhole shaping, ending with RS facing for next row.

Shape raglan armhole

Cast off 3 sts at beg of next row.
51 [56: 61: 66] sts.
Work 1 row.
Dec 1 st at raglan armhole edge of next and foll 13 [21: 27: 36] alt rows, then on every foll 4th [4th: 4th: 0] row until 27 [27: 29: 29] sts rem.
Work 0 [0: 2: 2] rows, ending with **WS** facing for next row.

Shape neck

Cast off 10 sts at beg of next row, then 8 sts at beg of foll alt row **and at same time** dec 0 [0: 1: 1] st at raglan armhole edge of 2nd row.
9 [9: 10: 10] sts.
Dec 1 st at neck edge of next 5 rows, then on foll 0 [0: 1: 1] alt row **and at same time** dec 1 st at raglan armhole edge of next [next: 3rd: 3rd] and foll 4th row. 2 sts.
Work 1 row, ending with RS facing for next row.
Next row (RS): K2tog and fasten off.

RIGHT FRONT

Work to match left front, reversing shapings.

SLEEVES

Using 4mm (US 6) needles cast on 44 [46: 48: 48] sts.
Beg with a K row, work in st st for 5 rows, ending with **WS** facing for next row.
Change to 4½mm (US 7) needles.
Work in g st, shaping sides by inc 1 st at each end of 4th [4th: 4th: 2nd] and every foll 10th [10th: 10th: 8th] row to 56 [66: 76: 58] sts, then on every foll 12th [12th: -: 10th] row until there are 68 [72: -: 78] sts.
Cont straight until sleeve meas 44 [45: 46: 46] cm **allowing first few rows to roll to RS**, ending with RS facing for next row.

Shape raglan

Cast off 3 sts at beg of next 2 rows.
62 [66: 70: 72] sts.
Dec 1 st at each end of next and every foll alt row to 34 sts, then on every foll 4th row until 10 sts rem.
Work 1 row, ending with RS facing for next row.
Left sleeve only
Work 1 row, then cast off 2 sts at beg of foll row.
8 sts.
Right sleeve only
Cast off 2 sts at beg of next row. 8 sts.
Work 1 row.
Both sleeves
Dec 1 st at cast-off (front neck) edge of next and foll 3 alt rows **and at same time** dec 1 st at back edge of next and foll 4th row.
Work 1 row, ending with RS facing for next row.
Next row (RS): K2tog and fasten off.

MAKING UP

Press as described on the information page.
Join all raglan seams using back stitch, or mattress stitch if preferred.
Front bands (both alike)
With RS facing and using 4mm (US 6) needles, pick up and knit 94 99: 101: 105] sts evenly along front opening edge, between neck shaping and cast-on edge.
Beg with a P row, work in st st for 5 rows, ending with RS facing for next row.
Cast off.
Collar
With RS facing and using 4mm (US 6) needles, beg and ending halfway across top of front bands, pick up and knit 27 [27: 30: 30] sts up right side of neck, 12 sts from right sleeve, 24 [24: 26: 26] sts from back, 12 sts from left sleeve, then 27 [27: 30: 30] sts down left side of neck.
102 [102: 110: 110] sts.
Row 1 (WS of body, RS of collar): P2, *K2, P2, rep from * to end.
Row 2: K2, *inc purlwise in each of next 2 sts, K2,

rep from * to end.

152 [152: 164: 164] sts.

Row 3: P2, *K4, P2, rep from * to end.

Row 4: K2, *P4, K2, rep from * to end.

Row 5: P2, *C4B, P2, rep from * to end.

Row 6: As row 4.

Rows 3 to 6 form patt.

Cont in patt until collar meas 21 cm from pick-up row, ending with RS facing for next row.

Cast off in patt.

See information page for finishing instructions.

Fasten fronts with decorative kilt pin as in photograph.

53 [55: 57: 59] cm
(21 [21¹/₂: 22¹/₂: 23] in)

48 [53.5: 59: 64.5] cm
(19 [21: 23: 25¹/₂] in)

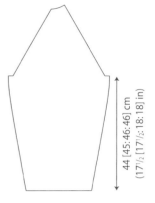

44 [45: 46: 46] cm
(17¹/₂ [17¹/₂: 18: 18] in)

Main image page 32

Hemlock

YARN

	S	M	L	XL	
To fit bust	81-86	91-97	102-107	112-117	cm
	32-34	36-38	40-42	44-46	in

RYC Natural Silk Aran

	11	12	14	16	x 50gm

(photographed in Charm 463)

NEEDLES

1 pair 4mm (no 8) (US 6) needles
1 pair 4½mm (no 7) (US 7) needles
4mm (no 8) (US 6) circular needle
Cable needle
1 yarn holder

TENSION

22 sts and 26 rows to 10 cm measured over cable pattern using 4½mm (US 7) needles. 18 sts and 34 rows to 10 cm measured over garter stitch using 4½mm (US 7) needles.

SPECIAL ABBREVIATIONS

C6F = slip next 4 sts onto cable needle and leave at front of work, K2, slip centre 2 sts (of this group of 6 sts) from cable needle back onto left needle and K these 2 sts, then K2 from cable needle.

BACK

Using 4mm (US 6) needles cast on 103 [113: 127: 141] sts.
Row 1 (RS): P10 [4: 11: 7], K1, K2tog, (yfwd) twice, sl 1, K1, psso, K1, *P5, K1, K2tog, (yfwd) twice, sl 1, K1, psso, K1, rep from * to last 10 [4: 11: 7] sts, P to end.
Row 2: K10 [4: 11: 7], P2, (K1, P1) into double yfwd of previous row, P2, *K5, P2, (K1, P1) into double yfwd of previous row, P2, rep from * to last 10 [4: 11: 7] sts, K to end.
Change to 4½mm (US 7) needles.
Row 3: P10 [4: 11: 7], K6, *P5, K6, rep from * to last 10 [4: 11: 7] sts, P to end.
Row 4: K10 [4: 11: 7], P6, *K5, P6, rep from * to last 10 [4: 11: 7] sts, K to end.
Row 5: P10 [4: 11: 7], C6F, *P5, C6F, rep from * to last 10 [4: 11: 7] sts, P to end.
Row 6: As row 4.
Rows 7 to 18: As rows 1 to 4, 3 times.

These 18 rows form cable patt.
Using 4½mm (US 7) needles **throughout**, cont in patt until back meas 36 [37: 38: 39] cm, ending with RS facing for next row.
Shape armholes
Keeping patt correct, cast off 8 [9: 10: 11] sts at beg of next 2 rows. 87 [95: 107: 119] sts.
Dec 1 st at each end of next row.
85 [93: 105: 117] sts.
Next row (WS): K7 [7: 5: 7], K2tog, (K2, K2tog) 17 [19: 23: 25] times, K to end. 67 [73: 81: 91] sts.
Cont in g st, dec 1 st at each end of next 1 [1: 3: 5] rows, then on foll 2 [3: 2: 3] alt rows, then on 2 foll 4th rows. 57 [61: 67: 71] sts.
Cont straight until armhole meas 20 [21: 22: 23] cm, ending with RS facing for next row.
Shape shoulders and back neck
Cast off 5 [6: 6: 7] sts at beg of next 2 rows.
47 [49: 55: 57] sts.
Next row (RS): Cast off 5 [6: 6: 7] sts, K until there are 9 [9: 11: 11] sts on right needle and turn, leaving rem sts on a holder.
Work each side of neck separately.
Cast off 4 sts at beg of next row.
Cast off rem 5 [5: 7: 7] sts.
With RS facing, rejoin yarn to rem sts, cast off centre 19 [19: 21: 21] sts, K to end.
Complete to match first side, reversing shapings.

LEFT FRONT

Using 4mm (US 6) needles cast on 52 [57: 64: 71] sts.
Row 1 (RS): P10 [4: 11: 7], K1, K2tog, (yfwd) twice, sl 1, K1, psso, K1, *P5, K1, K2tog, (yfwd) twice, sl 1, K1, psso, K1, rep from * to last 3 sts, P3.
Row 2: K3, P2, (K1, P1) into double yfwd of previous row, P2, *K5, P2, (K1, P1) into double yfwd of previous row, P2, rep from * to last 10 [4: 11: 7] sts, K to end.
Change to 4½mm (US 7) needles.
Row 3: P10 [4: 11: 7], K6, *P5, K6, rep from * to last 3 sts, P3.
Row 4: K3, P6, *K5, P6, rep from * to last 10 [4: 11: 7] sts, K to end.
Row 5: P10 [4: 11: 7], C6F, *P5, C6F, rep from * to last 3 sts, P3.
Row 6: As row 4.

Rows 7 to 18: As rows 1 to 4, 3 times.
These 18 rows form cable patt.
Using 4½mm (US 7) needles **throughout**, cont in patt until 32 rows less have been worked than on back to beg of armhole shaping, ending with RS facing for next row.
Shape front slope
Keeping patt correct, dec 1 st at end of next and 5 foll 6th rows. 46 [51: 58: 65] sts.
Work 1 row, ending with RS facing for next row.
Shape armhole
Keeping patt correct, cast off 8 [9: 10: 11] sts at beg of next row. 38 [42: 48: 54] sts.
Work 1 row.
Dec 1 st at beg of next row. 37 [41: 47: 53] sts.
Next row (WS): K3 [3: 2: 3], K2tog, (K2, K2tog) 7 [8: 10: 11] times, K to end. 29 [32: 36: 41] sts.
Cont in g st, dec 1 st at armhole edge of next 1 [1: 3: 5] rows, then on foll 2 [3: 2: 3] alt rows, then on 2 foll 4th rows **and at same time** dec 1 st at front slope edge of next and every foll 6th row. 21 [23: 26: 27] sts.
Dec 1 st at front slope edge **only** on 6th [4th: 4th: 6th] and 2 [0: 3: 0] foll 6th rows, then on every foll 8th row until 15 [17: 19: 21] sts rem.
Cont straight until left front matches back to beg of shoulder shaping, ending with RS facing for next row.
Shape shoulder
Cast off 5 [6: 6: 7] sts at beg of next and foll alt row.
Work 1 row.
Cast off rem 5 [5: 7: 7] sts.

RIGHT FRONT

Using 4mm (US 6) needles cast on 52 [57: 64: 71] sts.
Row 1 (RS): P3, K1, K2tog, (yfwd) twice, sl 1, K1, psso, K1, *P5, K1, K2tog, (yfwd) twice, sl 1, K1, psso, K1, rep from * to last 10 [4: 11: 7] sts, P to end.
Row 2: K10 [4: 11: 7], P2, (K1, P1) into double yfwd of previous row, P2, *K5, P2, (K1, P1) into double yfwd of previous row, P2, rep from * to last 3 sts, K3.
Change to 4½mm (US 7) needles.
Row 3: P3, K6, *P5, K6, rep from * to last 10 [4: 11: 7] sts, P to end.

Row 4: K10 [4: 11: 7], P6, *K5, P6, rep from * to last 3 sts, K3.

Row 5: P3, C6F, *P5, C6F, rep from * to last 10 [4: 11: 7] sts, P to end.

Row 6: As row 4.

Rows 7 to 18: As rows 1 to 4, 3 times.

These 18 rows form cable patt.

Complete to match left front, reversing shapings.

MAKING UP

Press as described on the information page.

Join both shoulder seams using back stitch, or mattress stitch if preferred.

Front band

With RS facing and using 4mm (US 6) circular needle, beg and ending at cast-on edges, pick up and knit 44 [46: 48: 50] sts up right front opening edge to beg of front slope shaping, 70 [72: 74: 76] sts up right front slope, 27 [27: 29: 29] sts from back, 70 [72: 74: 76] sts down left front slope to beg of front slope shaping, then 44 [46: 48: 50] sts down left front opening edge.

255 [263: 273: 281] sts.

Row 1 (WS): K44 [46: 48: 50], *turn, cast off 8 sts, turn, cast on 8 sts, turn (to make opening for tie)*, K to last 36 [38: 40: 42] sts, rep from * to * once more, K to end.

Work in g st for 5 rows, ending with **WS** facing for next row.

Cast off knitwise (on **WS**).

Armhole borders (both alike)

With RS facing and using 4mm (US 6) needles, pick up and knit 90 [96: 102: 108] sts evenly all round armhole edge.

Work in g st for 6 rows, ending with **WS** facing for next row.

Cast off knitwise (on **WS**).

Tie

Using 4mm (US 6) needles cast on 5 sts.

Work in g st until tie meas 61 cm.

Cast off.

See information page for finishing instructions.

Thread tie through openings and tie at centre front.

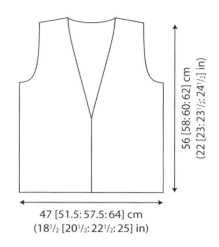

56 [58: 60: 62] cm
(22 [23: 23¹/₂: 24¹/₂] in)

47 [51.5: 57.5: 64] cm
(18¹/₂ [20¹/₂: 22¹/₂: 25] in)

Main image page 44

Honeysuckle

YARN

	1-2	2-3	3-4	4-5	years
To fit chest	56	58	61	64	cm
	22	23	24	25	in

RYC Cashcotton 4 ply

	3	3	4	4	x 50gm

(photographed in Peppermint 913)

NEEDLES

1 pair 2¾mm (no 12) (US 2) needles
1 pair 3¼mm (no 10) (US 3) needles
1 yarn holder

BEADS – approx 210 [250: 280: 330] beads
x 001022

TENSION

26½ sts and 36 rows to 10 cm measured over pattern using 3¼mm (US 3) needles.

SPECIAL ABBREVIATION

Bead 1 = place a bead by bringing yarn to RS of work and slipping bead up next to st just worked, slip next st purlwise from left needle to right needle and take yarn to WS of work, leaving bead sitting on RS of work in front of slipped st. Do not place beads on edge stitches of work as this will interfere with seaming.

Pattern note: Before starting to knit, thread beads onto yarn. To do this, thread a fine sewing needle (one that will easily pass through the beads) with sewing thread. Knot ends of thread and then pass end of yarn through this loop. Thread a bead onto sewing thread and then gently slide it along and onto knitting yarn. Continue in this way until required number of beads are on yarn.

BACK

Using 3¼mm (US 3) needles cast on 73 [77: 81: 85] sts.
Beg and ending rows as indicated and repeating the 12 row patt repeat throughout, cont in patt from chart as folls:
Work 6 rows, ending with RS facing for next row.
Inc 1 st at each end of next and every foll 4th [4th: 6th: 8th] row until there are 83 [87: 91: 95] sts, taking inc sts into patt.
Work 5 [9: 9: 5] rows, ending with RS facing for next row. (Back should meas 8 [9: 11: 12] cm.)
Shape armholes
Keeping patt correct, cast off 4 [5: 5: 6] sts at beg of next 2 rows.
75 [77: 81: 83] sts.
Dec 1 st at each end of next 3 rows, then on foll 2 [2: 3: 3] alt rows, then on foll 4th row.
63 [65: 67: 69] sts.
Cont straight until armhole meas 12 [13: 13: 14] cm, ending with RS facing for next row.
Shape shoulders and back neck
Next row (RS): Cast off 9 [9: 9: 10] sts, patt until there are 10 [11: 11: 11] sts on right needle and turn, leaving rem sts on a holder.
Work each side of neck separately.
Dec 1 st at beg of next row.

[chart diagram]

12
10

12 row patt rep

left front
1 - 2
2 - 3
3 - 4
4 - 5

1 - 2 sleeve
2 - 3 & 3 - 4 sleeve
4 - 5 sleeve

1 - 2
2 - 3
3 - 4
4 - 5
right front

Key

☐ K on RS, P on WS

☑ K2tog

◩ sl 1, K1, psso

◭ sl 1, K2tog, psso

◉ yfwd

▣ Bead1

Cast off rem 9 [10: 10: 10] sts.

With RS facing, rejoin yarn to rem sts, cast off centre 25 [25: 27: 27] sts, patt to end.

Complete to match first side, reversing shapings.

LEFT FRONT

Using 3¼mm (US 3) needles cast on 97 [99: 101: 103] sts.

Beg and ending rows as indicated, cont in patt from chart as folls:

Work 3 rows, ending with **WS** facing for next row.

Shape front slope

Keeping patt correct, cast off 5 sts at beg of next and foll 3 alt rows, then 9 sts at beg of foll 2 alt rows **and at same time** inc 1 st at beg of 4th and foll 4th [4th: 6th: 0] row, ending with RS facing for next row. 61 [63: 65: 66] sts.

Dec 1 st at front slope edge of next 14 [18: 17: 9] rows, then on foll 0 [0: 4: 10] alt rows **and at same time** inc 1 st at beg of next [next: 5th: next] and 2 [2: 2: 3] foll 4th [4th: 6th: 8th] rows. 50 [48: 47: 51] sts.

Work 0 [0: 1: 1] row, ending with RS facing for next row. (Left front should now match back to beg of armhole shaping.)

Shape armhole

Keeping patt correct, cast off 4 [5: 5: 6] sts at beg and dec 1 st at end of next row. 45 [42: 41: 44] sts.

Dec 1 [1: 0: 0] st at front slope edge of next row. 44 [41: 41: 44] sts.

Dec 1 st at armhole edge of next 3 rows, then on foll 2 [2: 3: 3] alt rows, then on foll 4th row **and at same time** dec 1 st at front slope edge of next 11 [1: 1: 1] rows, then on foll 0 [5: 6: 6] alt rows. 27 [29: 27: 30] sts.

Dec 1 st at front slope edge **only** on 2nd and foll 6 [7: 4: 6] alt rows, then on every foll 4th row until 18 [19: 19: 20] sts rem.

Cont straight until left front matches back to beg of shoulder shaping, ending with RS facing for next row.

Shape shoulder

Cast off 9 [9: 9: 10] sts at beg of next row.

Work 1 row.

Cast off rem 9 [10: 10: 10] sts.

RIGHT FRONT

Using 3¼mm (US 3) needles cast on 97 [99: 101: 103] sts.

Beg and ending rows as indicated, cont in patt from chart as folls:

Work 2 rows, ending with RS facing for next row.

Shape front slope

Keeping patt correct, cast off 5 sts at beg of next and foll 3 alt rows, then 9 sts at beg of foll 2 alt rows **and at same time** inc 1 st at beg of 5th and foll 4th [4th: 6th: 0] row, ending with RS facing for next row. 61 [63: 65: 66] sts.

Complete to match left front, reversing shapings.

SLEEVES

Using 3¼mm (US 3) needles cast on 49 [51: 51: 53] sts.

Beg and ending rows as indicated, cont in patt from chart, shaping sides by inc 1 st at each end of 15th [9th: 11th: 9th] and every foll 16th [12th: 12th: 10th] row to 53 [61: 59: 65] sts, then on every foll 18th [-: 14th: 12th] row until there are 55 [-: 61: 67] sts, taking inc sts into patt.

Cont straight until sleeve meas 18 [20: 22: 25] cm, ending with RS facing for next row.

Shape top

Keeping patt correct, cast off 4 [5: 5: 6] sts at beg of next 2 rows. 47 [51: 51: 55] sts.

Dec 1 st at each end of next 3 rows, then on foll 3 alt rows, then on every foll 4th row until 29 [33: 33: 37] sts rem.

Work 1 row.

Dec 1 st at each end of next and foll 0 [2: 2: 4] alt rows, then on foll 3 rows, ending with RS facing for next row.

Cast off rem 21 sts.

MAKING UP

Press as described on the information page.

Join both shoulder seams using back stitch, or mattress stitch if preferred.

See information page for finishing instructions, setting in sleeves using the set-in method.

Edging

Using 2¾mm (US 2) needles cast on 3 sts.

Row 1 (WS): P3.

Row 2: K1, yfwd, K1 tbl, P1. 4 sts.

Row 3: P2, (K1, P1, K1, P1) all into yfwd of previous row, P1.

7 sts.

Row 4: Cast off 4 sts (one st on right needle after cast-off), K1 tbl, P1. 3 sts.

These 4 rows form patt.

Cont in patt until edging fits around entire lower edge, front opening and back neck edges of body, ending after patt row 4 and with **WS** facing for next row.

Cast off (on **WS**).

Join cast-on and cast-off ends of edging, then slip st edging in place.

Work edging around lower edge of sleeves in same way.

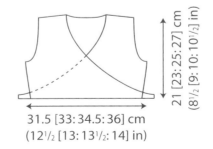

31.5 [33: 34.5: 36] cm
(12½ [13: 13½: 14] in)

21 [23: 25: 27] cm
(8½ [9: 10: 10½] in)

18 [20: 22: 25] cm
(7 [8: 8½: 10] in)

Main image page 46

Humbug Hood

YARN

	1-2	2-3	3-4	4-5	years
To fit chest	56	58	61	64	cm
	22	23	24	25	in

RYC Natural Silk Aran

| | 8 | 9 | 10 | 11 | x 50gm |

(photographed in Flax 461)

NEEDLES

1 pair 4mm (no 8) (US 6) needles
1 pair 4½mm (no 7) (US 7) needles
4mm (no 8) (US 6) circular needle
4½mm (no 7) (US 7) circular needle
2 double-pointed 4mm (no 8) (US 6) needles
2 yarn holders

TENSION

19 sts and 25 rows to 10 cm measured over stocking stitch using 4½mm (US 7) needles.

BACK

Using 4mm (US 6) needles cast on 59 [61: 65: 67] sts.
Beg with a K row, work in st st for 3 rows, ending with **WS** facing for next row.
Row 4 (WS): Knit (to form fold line).
Change to 4½mm (US 7) needles.**
Beg with a K row, cont in st st until back meas 16 [17: 19: 20] cm **from fold line row**, ending with RS facing for next row.
Shape raglan armholes
Cast off 2 sts at beg of next 2 rows.
55 [57: 61: 63] sts.

3-4 and 4-5 years only
Next row (RS): P2, K2tog, K to last 4 sts, sl 1, K1, psso, P2.
Next row: K2, P2tog tbl, P to last 4 sts, P2tog, K2.
– [-: 57: 59] sts.

All sizes
Next row (RS): P2, K2tog, K to last 4 sts, sl 1, K1, psso, P2.
Next row: K2, P to last 2 sts, K2.
Rep last 2 rows 17 [18: 17: 18] times more.
19 [19: 21: 21] sts.
Cast off.

FRONT

Work as given for back to **.
Beg with a K row, work in st st for 2 rows, ending with RS facing for next row.
Next row (eyelet row) (RS): K26 [27: 29: 30], K2tog, yfwd, K3, yfwd, sl 1, K1, psso, K to end.
Work 9 rows, ending with RS facing for next row.
Shape pocket
Next row (RS): K9 [10: 12: 13] and slip these sts onto a holder, K41 and turn, leaving rem 9 [10: 12: 13] sts on a second holder.
Work on this set of 41 sts only for pocket front.
Cast off 3 sts at beg of next 4 rows, ending with **WS** facing for next row. 29 sts.
Dec 1 st at each end of next 2 rows, then on foll alt row, then on 2 foll 4th rows. 19 sts.
Work 5 rows, ending with RS facing for next row.
Break yarn and leave rem 19 sts on another holder.
Rejoin yarn to sts left on second holder with RS facing and K to end.
Next row (WS): P9 [10: 12: 13], pick up and P41 sts across **WS** of first row of pocket front, P9 [10: 12: 13] sts from first holder.
59 [61: 65: 67] sts.
Work 21 rows, ending with RS facing for next row.
Join sections
Next row (RS): K first 20 [21: 23: 24] sts, now holding **WS** of pocket front against RS of work, K tog first st of pocket front with next st, (K tog next st of pocket front with next st) 18 times, K to end.
59 [61: 65: 67] sts.
Cont straight until front matches back to beg of raglan armhole shaping.
Shape raglan armholes
Cast off 2 sts at beg of next 2 rows.
55 [57: 61: 63] sts.
Working all raglan armhole decreases as set by back, dec 1 st at each end of next 1 [1: 3: 3] rows, then on every foll alt row until 29 [29: 33: 33] sts rem in raglan armhole shaping.
Work 1 row, ending with RS facing for next row.
Shape neck
Next row (RS): P2, K2tog, K2 [2: 4: 4] and turn, leaving rem sts on a holder.
Work each side of neck separately.

1-2 and 2-3 years only
Next row (WS): P2tog, P1, K2. 4 sts.

3-4 and 4-5 years only
Next row (WS): P2tog, P3, K2. 6 sts.
Next row: P2, (K2tog) twice. 4 sts.
Next row: P2, K2.

All sizes
Next row (RS): P1, P3tog.
Next row: K2.
Next row: P2tog and fasten off.
With RS facing, rejoin yarn to rem sts, cast off centre 17 sts, K to last 4 sts, sl 1, K1, psso, P2.
Complete to match first side, reversing shapings.

SLEEVES

Using 4mm (US 6) needles cast on 34 [34: 34: 38] sts.
Row 1 (RS): K2, *P2, K2, rep from * to end.
Row 2: P2, *K2, P2, rep from * to end.
These 2 rows form rib.
Work in rib for a further 6 rows, inc 0 [1: 1: 0] st at each end of last row and ending with RS facing for next row.
34 [36: 36: 38] sts.
Change to 4½mm (US 7) needles.
Beg with a K row, work in st st, shaping sides by inc 1 st at each end of 3rd and every foll alt [alt: alt: 4th] row to 42 [42: 40: 62] sts, then on every foll 4th [4th: 4th: -] row until there are 54 [58: 58: -] sts.
Cont straight until sleeve meas 20 [22: 24: 27] cm, ending with RS facing for next row.
Shape raglan
Cast off 2 sts at beg of next 2 rows.
50 [54: 54: 58] sts.

2-3, 3-4 and 4-5 years only
Next row (RS): P2, K2tog, K to last 4 sts, sl 1, K1, psso, P2.
Next row: K2, P2tog tbl, P to last 4 sts, P2tog, K2.
Rep last 2 rows – [0: 0: 1] times more.
– [50: 50: 50] sts.

All sizes
Next row (RS): P2, K2tog, K to last 4 sts, sl 1, K1,

psso, P2.

Next row: K2, P to last 2 sts, K2.

Working all raglan decreases as set by last 2 rows, dec 1 st at each end of next and every foll alt row until 20 sts rem.

Work 1 row, ending with RS facing for next row.

Keeping raglan decreases correct as set, cont as folls:

Left sleeve only

Dec 1 st at each end of next row, then cast off 3 sts at beg of foll row. 15 sts.

Dec 1 st at beg of next row, then cast off 4 sts at beg of foll row. 10 sts.

Rep last 2 rows once more.

Right sleeve only

Cast off 4 sts at beg and dec 1 st at end of next row. 15 sts.

Work 1 row.

Rep last 2 rows twice more.

Both sleeves

Cast off rem 5 sts.

MAKING UP

Press as described on the information page.

Join raglan seams using back stitch, or mattress stitch if preferred. Place markers on front neck cast-off edge 1.5 cm either side of centre front.

Hood

With RS facing and using 4½mm (US 7) circular needle, beg and ending at markers (and leaving centre front 3 cm free), pick up and knit 9 [9: 11: 11] sts up right side of neck, 15 sts from right sleeve, 21 [21: 23: 23] sts from back, 15 sts from left sleeve, then 9 [9: 11: 11] sts down left side of neck. 69 [69: 75: 75] sts.

Beg with P row, work in st st for 5 rows, ending with RS facing for next row.

Place marker on centre st of last row.

Next row (RS): K to marked st, M1, K marked st, M1, K to end. 71 [71: 77: 77] sts.

Work 3 rows.

Rep last 4 rows twice more, then first of these rows (the inc row) again. 77 [77: 83: 83] sts.

Cont straight until hood meas 23 [24: 24: 25] cm from pick-up row, ending with RS facing for next row.

Next row (RS): K to within 2 sts of marked st, sl 1, K1, psso, K marked st, K2tog, K to end.

Work 1 row.

Rep last 2 rows twice more, ending with RS facing for next row.

Cast off rem 71 [71: 77: 77] sts.

Fold hood in half and join cast-off edges to form top of hood seam.

Hood border

With RS facing and using 4mm (US 6) circular needle, beg and ending at markers on front neck, pick up and knit 102 [106: 106: 110] sts evenly along entire row-end edges of hood.

Beg with row 1, work in rib as given for sleeves for 4 rows, ending with **WS** facing for next row.

Cast off in rib (on **WS**).

Sew row-end edges of hood border to centre

front cast-off sts, so that cast-off edges of hood border meet at centre front.

Pocket borders (both alike)

With RS facing and using 4mm (US 6) needles, pick up and knit 26 sts evenly along shaped pocket opening edge.

Beg with row 1, work in rib as given for sleeves for 4 rows, ending with **WS** facing for next row.

Cast off in rib (on **WS**).

See information page for finishing instructions.

Fold first 3 rows of back and front to inside along fold line row and slip st in place.

Tie

Using double-pointed 4mm (US 6) needles cast on 2 sts.

Row 1 (RS): K2, *without turning slip these 2 sts to opposite end of needle and bring yarn to opposite end of work pulling it quite tightly across **WS** of work, K these 2 sts again, rep from * until tie is 81 [83: 86: 89] cm long, K2tog and fasten off.

Beg and ending at eyelet holes, thread tie through casing around lower edge and tie ends in a bow at centre front.

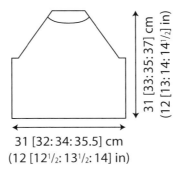

31 [32: 34: 35.5] cm
(12 [12½: 13½: 14] in)

31 [33:35: 37] cm
(12 [13: 14: 14½] in)

20 [22:24: 27] cm
(8 [8½: 9½: 10½] in)

Main image page 18

Liquorice Jacket

YARN

	1-2	2-3	3-4	4-5	years
To fit chest	56	58	61	64	cm
	22	23	24	25	in
RYC Natural Silk Aran					
A Black 465	5	5	6	6	x 50gm
B Flax 461	3	4	4	4	x 50gm

NEEDLES

1 pair 4mm (no 8) (US 6) needles
1 pair 4½mm (no 7) (US 7) needles
1 yarn holder

BUTTONS – 6 x 00406

TENSION

19 sts and 25 rows to 10 cm measured over stocking stitch using 4½mm (US 7) needles.

BACK

Using 4mm (US 6) needles and yarn A cast on 58 [60: 64: 66] sts.
Row 1 (RS): K0 [0: 1: 0], P0 [1: 2: 0], *K2, P2, rep from * to last 2 [3: 1: 2] sts, K2 [2: 1: 2], P0 [1: 0: 0].
Row 2: P0 [0: 1: 0], K0 [1: 2: 0], *P2, K2, rep from * to last 2 [3: 1: 2] sts, P2 [2: 1: 2], K0 [1: 0: 0].
These 2 rows form rib.
Cont in rib for a further 6 rows, ending with RS facing for next row.
Change to 4½mm (US 7) needles.
Join in yarn B.
Beg with a K row, work in striped st st as folls:
Using yarn B, work 6 rows.
Using yarn A, work 6 rows.
These 12 rows form striped st st.
Cont in striped st st until back meas 17 [18: 20: 21] cm, ending with RS facing for next row.
Shape armholes
Keeping stripes correct, cast off 3 sts at beg of next 2 rows. 52 [54: 58: 60] sts.
Dec 1 st at each end of next 2 rows.
48 [50: 54: 56] sts.
Cont straight until armhole meas 14 [15: 15: 16] cm, ending with RS facing for next row.
Shape shoulders and back neck
Next row (RS): Cast off 7 [7: 8: 8] sts, K until there are 8 [9: 9: 10] sts on right needle and turn,

leaving rem sts on a holder.
Work each side of neck separately.
Dec 1 st at beg of next row.
Cast off rem 7 [8: 8: 9] sts.
With RS facing, rejoin appropriate yarn to rem sts, cast off centre 18 [18: 20: 20] sts, K to end.
Complete to match first side, reversing shapings.

POCKET LININGS (make 2)

Using 4½mm (US 7) needles and yarn A cast on 17 [17: 18: 18] sts.
Beg with a K row, work in st st for 18 rows, ending with RS facing for next row.
Break yarn and leave sts on a holder.

LEFT FRONT

Using 4mm (US 6) needles and yarn A cast on 29 [30: 32: 33] sts.
Row 1 (RS): K0 [0: 1: 0], P0 [1: 2: 0], *K2, P2, rep from * to last st, K1.
Row 2: P1, K2, *P2, K2, rep from * to last 2 [3: 1: 2] sts, P2 [2: 1: 2], K0 [1: 0: 0].
These 2 rows form rib.
Cont in rib for a further 6 rows, ending with RS facing for next row.
Change to 4½mm (US 7) needles.
Join in yarn B.
Beg with a K row and 6 rows using yarn B, work in striped st st as given for back for 18 rows, ending with RS facing for next row.
Place pocket
Next row (RS): K6 [7: 8: 9], slip next 17 [17: 18: 18] sts onto a holder and, in their place, K across 17 [17: 18: 18] sts of first pocket lining, K6.
Cont straight until left front matches back to beg of armhole shaping, ending with RS facing for next row.
Shape armhole
Keeping stripes correct, cast off 3 sts at beg of next row. 26 [27: 29: 30] sts.
Work 1 row.
Dec 1 st at armhole edge of next 2 rows.
24 [25: 27: 28] sts.
Cont straight until 5 [5: 7: 7] rows less have been worked than on back to beg of shoulder shaping, ending with **WS** facing for next row.
Shape neck
Keeping stripes correct, cast off 7 sts at beg of

next row. 17 [18: 20: 21] sts.
Dec 1 st at neck edge of next 3 rows, then on foll 0 [0: 1: 1] alt row. 14 [15: 16: 17] sts.
Work 1 row, ending with RS facing for next row.
Shape shoulder
Cast off 7 [7: 8: 8] sts at beg of next row.
Work 1 row.
Cast off rem 7 [8: 8: 9] sts.

RIGHT FRONT

Using 4mm (US 6) needles and yarn A cast on 29 [30: 32: 33] sts.
Row 1 (RS): K1, P2, *K2, P2, rep from * to last 2 [3: 1: 2] sts, K2 [2: 1: 2], P0 [1: 0: 0].
Row 2: P0 [0: 1: 0], K0 [1: 2: 0], *P2, K2, rep from * to last st, P1.
These 2 rows form rib.
Cont in rib for a further 6 rows, ending with RS facing for next row.
Change to 4½mm (US 7) needles.
Join in yarn B.
Beg with a K row and 6 rows using yarn B, work in striped st st as given for back for 18 rows, ending with RS facing for next row.
Place pocket
Next row (RS): K6, slip next 17 [17: 18: 18] sts onto a holder and, in their place, K across 17 [17: 18: 18] sts of second pocket lining, K6 [7: 8: 9].
Complete to match left front, reversing shapings.

SLEEVES

Using 4mm (US 6) needles and yarn A cast on 34 [36: 36: 38] sts.
Row 1 (RS): P0 [1: 1: 2], *K2, P2, rep from * to last 2 [3: 3: 4] sts, K2, P0 [1: 1: 2].
Row 2: K0 [1: 1: 2], *P2, K2, rep from * to last 2 [3: 3: 4] sts, P2, K0 [1: 1: 2].
These 2 rows form rib.
Cont in rib for a further 6 rows, ending with RS facing for next row.
Change to 4½mm (US 7) needles.
Join in yarn B.
Beg with a K row and 6 rows using yarn B, work in striped st st as given for back, shaping sides by inc 1 st at each end of next and every foll 4th row to 54 [58: 54: 54] sts, then on every foll - [-: 6th: 6th] row until there are - [-: 58: 62] sts.
Cont straight until sleeve meas 20 [22: 24: 27] cm,

ending with RS facing for next row.

Shape top

Keeping stripes correct, cast off 3 sts at beg of next 2 rows.

48 [52: 52: 56] sts.

Dec 1 st at each end of next and foll 2 alt rows, ending with **WS** facing for next row.

Cast off rem 42 [46: 46: 50] sts (on **WS**).

MAKING UP

Press as described on the information page.

Join both shoulder seams using back stitch, or mattress stitch if preferred.

Right front band and collar

Using 4mm (US 6) needles and yarn A cast on 6 sts. Work in g st until right front band, when slightly stretched, fits up right front opening edge to beg of neck shaping, ending with RS facing for next row.

Shape collar

Inc 1 st at end of next row and at same edge of every row until there are 32 sts.

Cont straight until collar, unstretched, fits up right front neck and across to centre back neck, ending with RS of collar (**WS** of front band) facing for next row.

Cast off 10 sts at beg of next and foll alt row.

Work 1 row.

Cast off rem 12 sts.

Slip st band and collar in place.

Mark positions for 6 buttons on this band – first

to come 1 cm up from cast-on edge, last to come just below neck shaping, and rem 4 buttons evenly spaced between.

Left front band and collar

Using 4mm (US 6) needles and yarn A cast on 6 sts. Work in g st until left front band, when slightly stretched, fits up left front opening edge to beg of neck shaping, ending with RS facing for next row and with the addition of 6 buttonholes to correspond with positions marked for buttons worked as folls:

Buttonhole row (RS): K1, K2tog, yfwd, K3.

Shape collar

Inc 1 st at beg of next row and at same edge of every row until there are 32 sts.

Cont straight until collar, unstretched, fits up left front neck and across to centre back neck, ending

with **WS** of collar (RS of front band) facing for next row.

Cast off 10 sts at beg of next and foll alt row.

Work 1 row.

Cast off rem 12 sts.

Slip st band and collar in place, joining cast-off edges at centre back neck.

Pocket tops (both alike)

Slip 17 [17: 18: 18] sts left on pocket holder onto 4mm (US 6) needles and rejoin yarn A with RS facing.

Work in g st for 5 rows, ending with **WS** facing for next row.

Cast off knitwise (on **WS**).

See information page for finishing instructions, setting in sleeves using the shallow set-in method.

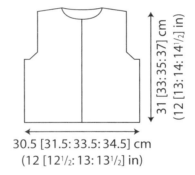

31 [33: 35: 37] cm
(12 [13: 14: 14¹/₂] in)

30.5 [31.5: 33.5: 34.5] cm
(12 [12¹/₂: 13: 13¹/₂] in)

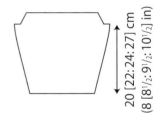

20 [22: 24: 27] cm
(8 [8¹/₂: 9¹/₂: 10¹/₂] in)

Main image page 19

 Liquorice Beanie

YARN

		1-3	3-5	years
RYC Natural Silk Aran				
A Black	465	1	2	x 50gm
B Flax	461	1	2	x 50gm

NEEDLES

1 pair 4½mm (no 7) (US 7) needles

TENSION

19 sts and 25 rows to 10 cm measured over stocking stitch using 4½mm (US 7) needles.

BEANIE

Using 4½mm (US 7) needles and yarn A cast on 82 [91] sts.
Beg with a K row, work in striped st st as folls:
Using yarn A, work 6 rows.
Join in yarn B.
Using yarn B, work 6 rows.
These 12 rows form striped st st.
Cont in striped st st until beanie meas 12 [13] cm, ending with RS facing for next row.

Shape crown

Keeping stripes correct, cont as folls:
Row 1 (RS): K1, *K2tog, K7, rep from * to end.
73 [81] sts.
Row 2 and every foll alt row: Purl.
Row 3: K1, *K2tog, K6, rep from * to end.
64 [71] sts.
Row 5: K1, *K2tog, K5, rep from * to end. 55 [61] sts.
Row 7: K1, *K2tog, K4, rep from * to end. 46 [51] sts.
Row 9: K1, *K2tog, K3, rep from * to end.
37 [41] sts.
Row 11: K1, *K2tog, K2, rep from * to end.
28 [31] sts.
Row 13: K1, *K2tog, K1, rep from * to end.
Row 14: Purl.
Break yarn and thread through rem 19 [21] sts.
Pull up tight and fasten off securely.

MAKING UP

Press as described on the information page.
Join back seam using back stitch, or mattress stitch if preferred, reversing seam for first few rows for st st roll.

Main image page 38

Sampler Blanket

YARN
RYC Cashsoft DK
6   x 50gm
(photographed in Cream 500)

NEEDLES
1 pair 4mm (no 8) (US 6) needles

TENSION
22 sts and 34 rows to 10 cm measured over
pattern using 4mm (US 6) needles.

FINISHED SIZE
Completed blanket measures 60 cm (23½ in)
wide and 81 cm (32 in) long.

PANELS (make 20)
Using 4mm (US 6) needles cast on 33 sts.
Work in patt from chart until all 55 rows have been
completed, ending with **WS** facing for next row.
Cast off knitwise (on **WS**).

MAKING UP
Press as described on the information page.
Using photograph as a guide, join panels to form
one large rectangle 4 panels wide and 5 panels
long.

Key

☐ K on RS,
   P on WS

▣ P on RS,
   K on WS

Main image page 30

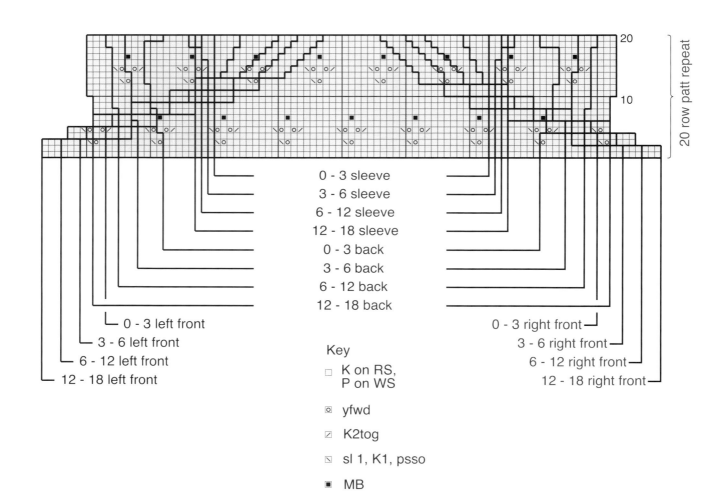

Lollipop

YARN

	0-3	3-6	6-12	12-18	months
To fit chest	41	46	51	56	cm
	16	18	20	22	in

RYC Cashcotton 4 ply

	2	3	3	4	x 50gm

(photographed in Citron 917)

NEEDLES

1 pair 2¾mm (no 12) (US 2) needles
1 pair 3¼mm (no 10) (US 3) needles
1 yarn holder

TENSION

28 sts and 36 rows to 10 cm measured over pattern using 3¼mm (US 3) needles.

SPECIAL ABBREVIATIONS

MB = (K1, P1, K1) all into next st, turn, P3, turn, sl 1, K2tog, psso.

BACK

Using 3¼mm (US 3) needles cast on 59 [67: 73: 81] sts.
Beg and ending rows as indicated and repeating the 20 row patt repeat throughout, cont in patt from chart as folls:
Inc 1 st at each end of 5th [7th: 9th: 11th] and every foll 4th [8th: 10th: 12th] row until there are 65 [73: 79: 87] sts, taking inc sts into patt.
Work 5 [5: 11: 15] rows, ending with RS facing for next row.
(Back should meas 5 [8: 11: 14] cm.)

Shape armholes

Keeping patt correct, cast off 3 [4: 4: 5] sts at beg of next 2 rows. 59 [65: 71: 77] sts.
Dec 1 st at each end of next 3 rows, then on foll 3 alt rows. 47 [53: 59: 65] sts.

0 - 3 sleeve
3 - 6 sleeve
6 - 12 sleeve
12 - 18 sleeve
0 - 3 back
3 - 6 back
6 - 12 back
12 - 18 back

0 - 3 left front
3 - 6 left front
6 - 12 left front
12 - 18 left front

0 - 3 right front
3 - 6 right front
6 - 12 right front
12 - 18 right front

20 row patt repeat

Key

□ K on RS, P on WS

⊙ yfwd

☑ K2tog

◩ sl 1, K1, psso

■ MB

Cont straight until armhole meas 9 [10: 11: 12] cm, ending with RS facing for next row.

Shape shoulders and back neck

Next row (RS): Cast off 5 [6: 7: 8] sts, patt until there are 6 [7: 8: 9] sts on right needle and turn, leaving rem sts on a holder.

Work each side of neck separately.

Dec 1 st at neck edge of next row.

Cast off rem 5 [6: 7: 8] sts.

With RS facing, rejoin yarn to rem sts, cast off centre 25 [27: 29: 31] sts, patt to end.

Complete to match first side, reversing shapings.

LEFT FRONT

Using 3¼mm (US 3) needles cast on 68 [76: 82: 89] sts.

Beg and ending rows as indicated, cont in patt from chart as folls:

Work 3 rows, ending with **WS** facing for next row.

Shape front slope

Keeping patt correct, cast off 4 sts at beg of next and foll alt rows, then 6 sts at beg of foll 2 alt rows, then 4 sts at beg of foll 2 alt rows **and at same time** inc 1 st at beg of 2nd [4th: 6th: 8th] and 2 [0: 0: 0] foll 4th rows.

43 [49: 55: 62] sts.

Dec 1 st at front slope edge of next 4 [14: 7: 1] rows, then on foll 0 [0: 9: 17] alt rows **and at same time** inc 0 [1: 1: 1] st at beg of – [next: 5th: 9th] and foll – [8th: 10th: 12th] row.

39 [37: 41: 46] sts.

Work 0 [0: 1: 1] row, ending with RS facing for next row. (Left front should now match back to beg of armhole shaping.)

Shape armholes

Keeping patt correct, cast off 3 [4: 4: 5] sts at beg and dec 1 st at end of next row. 35 [32: 36: 40] sts.

Dec 1 st at front slope edge of next [2nd: 2nd: 2nd] and foll 13 [0: 0: 0] rows, then on foll 5 [13: 15: 17] alt rows **and at same time** dec 1 st at armhole edge of next 3 rows, then on foll 3 alt rows. 10 [12: 14: 16] sts.

Cont straight until left front matches back to beg of shoulder shaping, ending with RS facing for next row.

Shape shoulder

Cast off 5 [6: 7: 8] sts at beg of next row.

Work 1 row.

Cast off rem 5 [6: 7: 8] sts.

RIGHT FRONT

Using 3¼mm (US 3) needles cast on 68 [76: 82: 89] sts.

Beg and ending rows as indicated, cont in patt from chart as folls:

Work 2 rows, ending with RS facing for next row.

Shape front slope

Keeping patt correct, cast off 4 sts at beg of next and foll alt rows, then 6 sts at beg of foll 2 alt rows, then 4 sts at beg of foll 2 alt rows **and at same time** inc 1 st at beg of 3rd [5th: 7th: 9th] and 2 [0: 0: 0] foll 4th rows. 43 [49: 55: 62] sts.

Complete to match left front, reversing shapings.

SLEEVES

Using 3¼mm (US 3) needles cast on 43 [45: 47: 49] sts.

Beg and ending rows as indicated, cont in patt from chart, shaping sides by inc 1 st at each end of 21st [17th: 19th: 19th] and every foll 22nd [18th: 22nd: 20th] row until there are 47 [51: 53: 57] sts, taking inc sts into patt.

Cont straight until sleeve meas 15 [18: 22: 26] cm, ending with RS facing for next row.

Shape top

Keeping patt correct, cast off 3 [4: 4: 5] sts at beg of next 2 rows. 41 [43: 45: 47] sts.

Dec 1 st at each end of next 3 rows, then on every foll alt row until 25 sts rem, then on 5 foll rows, ending with RS facing for next row.

Cast off rem 15 sts.

MAKING UP

Press as described on the information page.

See information page for finishing instructions, setting in sleeves using the set-in method.

Edging

Using 2¾mm (US 2) needles cast on 3 sts.

Row 1 (WS): P3.

Row 2: K1, yfwd, K1 tbl, P1. 4 sts.

Row 3: P2, (K1, P1, K1, P1) all into yfwd of previous row, P1. 7 sts.

Row 4: Cast off 4 sts (one st on right needle after cast-off), K1 tbl, P1. 3 sts.

These 4 rows form patt.

Cont in patt until edging fits around entire lower edge, front opening and back neck edges of body, ending after patt row 4 and with **WS** facing for next row.

Cast off (on **WS**).

Join cast-on and cast-off ends of edging, then slip st edging in place.

Work edging around lower edge of sleeves in same way.

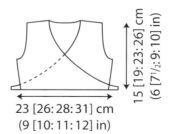

23 [26: 28: 31] cm
(9 [10: 11: 12] in)

15 [19: 23: 26] cm
(6 [7½: 9: 10] in)

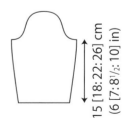

15 [18: 22: 26] cm
(6 [7: 8½: 10] in)

Main image page 22

 **May**

YARN

	S	M	L	XL	
To fit bust	81-86	91-97	102-107	112-117	cm
	32-34	36-38	40-42	44-46	in

RYC Cashsoft DK

	6	7	8	9	x 50gm

(photographed in Tape 515)

NEEDLES

1 pair 3¼mm (no 10) (US 3) needles
1 pair 4mm (no 8) (US 6) needles
Cable needle
2 double-pointed 3¼mm (no 10) (US 3) needles

TENSION

26 sts and 30 rows to 10 cm measured over pattern using 4mm (US 6) needles.

SPECIAL ABBREVIATIONS

Cr4R = slip next st onto cable needle and leave at back of work, K3, then P1 from cable needle;
Cr4L = slip next 3 sts onto cable needle and leave at front of work, P1, then K3 from cable needle; **C7B** = slip next 4 sts onto cable needle and leave at back of work, K3, then K4 from cable needle; **MB** = (K1, P1, K1, P1, K1) all into next st, turn, P5, turn, K5, turn, P2tog, P1, P2tog, turn, sl 1, K2tog, psso.

BACK

Using 3¼mm (US 3) needles cast on 101 [113: 123: 139] sts.
Work in g st for 5 rows, ending with **WS** facing for next row.
Row 6 (WS): K11 [17: 7: 15], M1, (K2, M1) twice, *K11, M1, (K2, M1) twice, rep from * 4 [4: 6: 6] times more, K to end. 119 [131: 147: 163] sts.
Change to 4mm (US 6) needles.
Beg and ending rows as indicated and repeating the 12 row patt repeat throughout, cont in patt from chart as folls:
Cont straight until back meas 8 [9: 10: 11] cm, ending with RS facing for next row.
Shape raglan armholes
Keeping patt correct, cast off 2 sts at beg of next 2 rows. 115 [127: 143: 159] sts.

Dec 1 st at each end of next 1 [9: 21: 33] rows, then on every foll alt row until 33 [33: 35: 35] sts rem.
Work 1 row, ending with RS facing for next row.
Cast off.

LEFT FRONT

Using 3¼mm (US 3) needles cast on 51 [57: 62: 70] sts.
Work in g st for 5 rows, ending with **WS** facing for next row.
Row 6 (WS): K6, M1, (K2, M1) twice, *K11, M1, (K2, M1) twice, rep from * 1 [1: 2: 2] times more, K to end. 60 [66: 74: 82] sts.
Change to 4mm (US 6) needles.
Beg and ending rows as indicated, cont in patt from chart as folls:
Cont straight until left front matches back to beg of raglan armhole shaping, ending with RS facing for next row.
Shape raglan armhole and front slope
Keeping patt correct, cast off 2 sts at beg and dec 1 st at end of next row. 57 [63: 71: 79] sts.

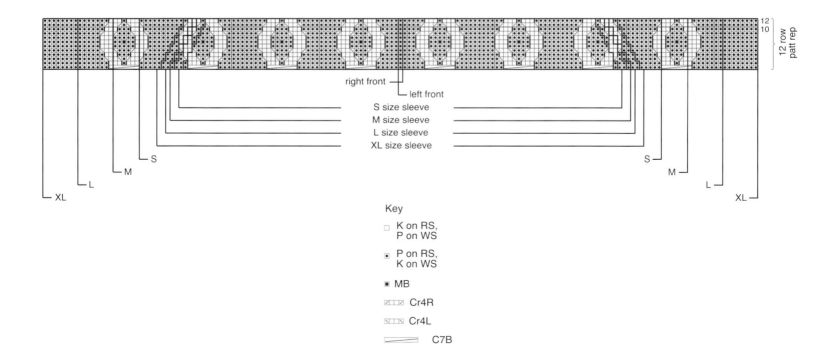

12
10

12 row patt rep

right front
left front
S size sleeve
M size sleeve
L size sleeve
XL size sleeve

S
M
S
L
M
XL
L
XL

Key

☐ K on RS, P on WS

▫ P on RS, K on WS

▪ MB

▨ Cr4R

▨ Cr4L

▭ C7B

Work 1 row.

Dec 1 st at raglan armhole edge of next 1 [9: 21: 33] rows, then on foll 34 [32: 27: 23] alt rows **and at same time** dec 1 st at front slope edge of next and foll 5 [3: 4: 2] alt rows, then on every foll 4th row. 2 sts.

Work 1 row, ending with RS facing for next row.

Next row (RS): P2tog and fasten off.

RIGHT FRONT

Using 3¼mm (US 3) needles cast on 51 [57: 62: 70] sts.

Work in g st for 5 rows, ending with **WS** facing for next row.

Row 6 (WS): K11 [17: 7: 15], M1, (K2, M1) twice, *K11, M1, (K2, M1) twice, rep from * 1 [1: 2: 2] times more, K to end. 60 [66: 74: 82] sts.

Complete to match left front, reversing shapings.

SLEEVES

Using 3¼mm (US 3) needles cast on 95 [99: 101: 105] sts.

Work in g st for 2 rows, ending with RS facing for next row.

Shape raglan

Cast off 2 sts at beg of next 2 rows.

91 [95: 97: 101] sts.

Dec 1 st at each end of next row.

89 [93: 95: 99] sts.

Row 6 (WS): K20 [22: 23: 25], M1, (K2, M1) twice, *K11, M1, (K2, M1) twice, rep from * twice more, K to end. 101 [105: 107: 111] sts.

Change to 4mm (US 6) needles.

Beg and ending rows as indicated, cont in patt from chart as folls:

Dec 1 st at each end of next and every foll alt row until 33 sts rem.

Work 1 row, ending with RS facing for next row.

Left sleeve only

Dec 1 st at each end of next row, then cast off 3 sts at beg of foll row. 28 sts.

Dec 1 st at beg of next row, then cast off 3 sts at beg of foll row. 24 sts.

Rep last 2 rows once more. 20 sts.

Dec 1 st at beg of next row, then cast off 4 sts at beg of foll row. 15 sts.

Right sleeve only

Cast off 4 sts at beg and dec 1 st at end of next row. 28 sts.

Work 1 row.

Cast off 3 sts at beg and dec 1 st at end of next row. 24 sts.

Work 1 row.

Rep last 2 rows once more. 20 sts.

Cast off 4 sts at beg and dec 1 st at end of next row. 15 sts.

Work 1 row.

Both sleeves

Rep last 2 rows twice more.

Cast off rem 5 sts.

MAKING UP

Press as described on the information page. Join all raglan seams using back stitch, or mattress stitch if preferred.

Left front band and collar

Using 3¼mm (US 3) needles cast on 7 sts.

Work in g st until left front band, when slightly stretched, fits up left front opening edge to beg of front slope shaping, ending with RS facing for next row.

Shape collar

Inc 1 st at beg of next and foll 20 alt rows, then on every foll 4th row until there are 48 sts.

Cont straight until collar, unstretched, fits up left front slope, across top of left sleeve and across to centre back neck, ending with **WS** of collar (RS of front band) facing for next row.

Cast off 12 sts at beg of next and foll 2 alt rows.

Work 1 row.

Cast off rem 12 sts.

Slip st band and collar in place.

Right front band and collar

Work to match left front band and collar, reversing shapings.

Slip st band and collar in place, joining cast-off edges at centre back neck.

See information page for finishing instructions.

Ties (make 2)

Using double-pointed 3¼mm (US 3) needles cast on 3 sts.

Row 1 (RS): K3, *without turning slip these 3 sts to opposite end of needle and bring yarn to opposite end of work pulling it quite tightly across **WS** of work, K these 3 sts again, rep from * until tie is 26 cm long, K3tog and fasten off.

Attach ties to front opening edges level with beg of front slope shaping.

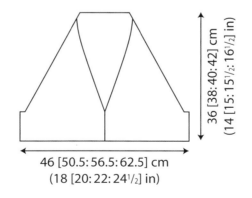

36 [38: 40: 42] cm
(14 [15: 15½: 16½] in)

46 [50.5: 56.5: 62.5] cm
(18 [20: 22: 24½] in)

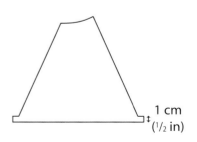

1 cm
(½ in)

Main image page 36

 Nougat

YARN

	0-3	3-6	6-12	12-18	months
To fit chest	41	46	51	56	cm
	16	18	20	22	in
RYC Cashsoft DK					
	3	4	5	6	x 50gm

(photographed in Mist 505)

NEEDLES

1 pair 3¼mm (no 10) (US 3) needles
1 pair 4mm (no 8) (US 6) needles
3¼mm (no 10) (US 3) circular needle

BUTTONS – 6 x 00405

TENSION

22 sts and 34 rows to 10 cm measured over
pattern using 4mm (US 6) needles.

BACK

Using 3¼mm (US 3) needles cast on 55 [61:
67: 73] sts.
Row 1 (RS): Ko [2: 0: 2], P2 [3: 2: 3], *K3, P3,
rep from * to last 5 [2: 5: 2] sts, K3 [2: 3: 2], P2 [0:
2: 0].
Row 2: Po [2: 0: 2], K2 [3: 2: 3], *P3, K3, rep from
* to last 5 [2: 5: 2] sts, P3 [2: 3: 2], K2 [0: 2: 0].
These 2 rows form rib.
Work in rib for a further 2 rows, ending with RS
facing for next row.
Change to 4mm (US 6) needles.
Cont in patt as folls:
Row 1 (RS): Knit.
Row 2: Purl.
Rows 3 to 6: Knit.
These 6 rows form patt.
Cont in patt until back meas 13 [16: 19: 22] cm,
ending with RS facing for next row.
Shape raglan armholes
Keeping patt correct, cast off 2 sts at beg of next
2 rows. 51 [57: 63: 69] sts.
Dec 1 st at each end of next and every foll alt row
until 19 [21: 23: 25] sts rem.
Work 1 row, ending with RS facing for next row.
Cast off rem 19 [21: 23: 25] sts.
Mark levels for buttonholes along one side seam
– lowest buttonhole in first rep of patt row 3, top
buttonhole just below beg of raglan armhole
shaping, and rem buttonhole evenly spaced
between.

LEFT FRONT

Using 3¼mm (US 3) needles cast on 38 [41:
44: 47] sts.
Row 1 (RS): Ko [2: 0: 2], P2 [3: 2: 3], *K3, P3, rep
from * to end.
Row 2: K3, *P3, K3, rep from * to last 5 [2: 5: 2] sts,
P3 [2: 3: 2], K2 [0: 2: 0].
These 2 rows form rib.
Work in rib for a further 2 rows, ending with RS
facing for next row.
Change to 4mm (US 6) needles.
Beg with patt row 1, work in patt as given for
back as folls:
For a girl
Cont in patt until left front matches back to beg
of raglan armhole shaping, ending with RS facing
for next row.
For a boy
Beg with patt row 1, work in patt as given for back
for 2 rows, ending with RS facing for next row.
Next row (buttonhole row) (RS): Patt to last 19 sts,
yrn, work 2 tog (to make first buttonhole of first
pair), patt to last 3 sts, yrn, work 2 tog (to make
2nd buttonhole of first pair), patt 1 st.
Cont in patt until left front matches back to beg
of raglan armhole shaping, making a further
2 pairs of buttonholes as before to correspond
with levels marked on back for buttonholes and
ending with RS facing for next row.
For a girl or a boy
Shape raglan armhole and front slope
Keeping patt correct, cast off 2 sts at beg and dec
1 st at end of next row. 35 [38: 41: 44] sts.
Dec 1 st at beg of next row and at same edge on
foll 9 [7: 5: 3] rows, then on foll 9 [12: 15: 18] alt
rows and at same time dec 1 st at raglan armhole
edge of 2nd and every foll alt row. 2 sts.
Work 1 row, ending with RS facing for next row.
Next row (RS): K2tog and fasten off.

RIGHT FRONT

Using 3¼mm (US 3) needles cast on 38 [41:
44: 47] sts.
Row 1 (RS): P3, *K3, P3, rep from * to last 5 [2:
5: 2] sts, K3 [2: 3: 2], P2 [0: 2: 0].

Row 2: Po [2: 0: 2], K2 [3: 2: 3], *P3, K3, rep from
* to end.
These 2 rows form rib.
Work in rib for a further 2 rows, ending with RS
facing for next row.
Change to 4mm (US 6) needles.
Beg with patt row 1, work in patt as given for
back as folls:
For a girl
Beg with patt row 1, work in patt as given for
back for 2 rows, ending with RS facing for next
row.
Next row (buttonhole row) (RS): Patt 1 st, work
2 tog, yrn (to make first buttonhole of first pair),
patt 14 sts, work 2 tog, yrn (to make 2nd
buttonhole of first pair), patt to end.
Cont in patt until right front matches back to beg
of raglan armhole shaping, making a further
2 pairs of buttonholes as before to correspond
with levels marked on back for buttonholes and
ending with RS facing for next row.
For a boy
Cont in patt until right front matches back to beg
of raglan armhole shaping, ending with RS facing
for next row.
For a girl or a boy
Complete to match left front, reversing shapings.

SLEEVES

Using 3¼mm (US 3) needles cast on 33 [35:
37: 39] sts.
Row 1 (RS): Ko [1: 2: 3], *P3, K3, rep from * to last
3 [4: 5: 6] sts, P3, Ko [1: 2: 3].
Row 2: Po [1: 2: 3], *K3, P3, rep from * to last
3 [4: 5: 6] sts, K3, Po [1: 2: 3].
These 2 rows form rib.
Work in rib for a further 2 rows, ending with RS
facing for next row.
Change to 4mm (US 6) needles.
Beg with patt row 1, cont in patt as given for
back, shaping sides by inc 1 st at each end of 3rd
and every foll 4th [4th: 4th: 6th] row to 51 [47:
45: 63] sts, then on every foll - [6th: 6th: -] row
until there are - [55: 59: -] sts.
Cont straight until sleeve meas approx 15 [18:
22: 26] cm, ending after same patt row as on
back to beg of raglan armhole shaping and with
RS facing for next row.

Shape raglan

Keeping patt correct, cast off 2 sts at beg of next 2 rows. 47 [51: 55: 59] sts.

Dec 1 st at each end of next and every foll alt row until 19 sts rem.

Work 1 row, ending with RS facing for next row.

Left sleeve only

Dec 1 st at each end of next row, then cast off 4 sts at beg of foll row. 13 sts.

Dec 1 st at beg of next row, then cast off 6 sts at beg of foll row.

Right sleeve only

Cast off 5 sts at beg and dec 1 st at end of next row. 13 sts.

Work 1 row.

Cast off 6 sts at beg and dec 1 st at end of next row.

Work 1 row.

Both sleeves

Cast off rem 6 sts.

MAKING UP

Press as described on the information page.

Join all raglan seams using back stitch, or mattress stitch if preferred.

Front band

With RS facing and using 3¼mm (US 3) circular needle, beg and ending at cast-on edges, pick up and knit 36 [43: 49: 56] sts up right front opening edge to beg of front slope shaping, 26 [30: 33: 37] sts up right front slope, 12 sts from right sleeve, 18 [20: 22: 24] sts from back, 12 sts from left sleeve, 26 [30: 33: 37] sts down left front slope to beg of front slope shaping, then 36 [43: 49: 56] sts down left front opening edge. 166 [190: 210: 234] sts.

Row 1 (WS): P2, *K2, P2, rep from * to end.

Row 2: K2, *P2, K2, rep from * to end.

These 2 rows form rib.

Work in rib for a further 2 rows, ending with **WS** facing for next row.

Cast off in rib (on **WS**).

See information page for finishing instructions.

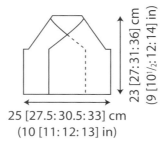

25 [27.5: 30.5: 33] cm
(10 [11: 12: 13] in)

23 [27: 31: 36] cm
(9 [10½: 12: 14] in)

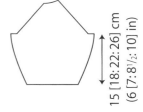

15 [18: 22: 26] cm
(6 [7: 8½: 10] in)

Main image page 42

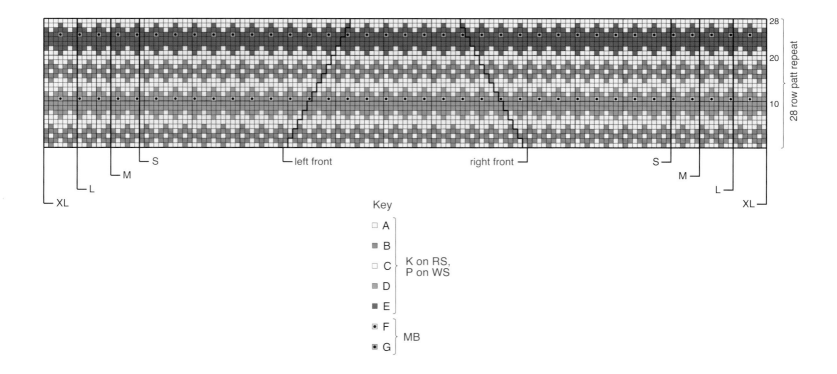

Penny Gilet

YARN

		S	M	L	XL	
To fit bust		81-86	91-97	102-107	112-117	cm
		32-34	36-38	40-42	44-46	in
RYC Cashsoft DK						
A Savannah	507	7	8	9	11	x 50gm
B Poison	513	2	2	3	3	x 50gm
C Mist	505	1	1	1	1	x 50gm
D Kingfisher	525	2	2	2	2	x 50gm
E Navy	514	2	2	2	2	x 50gm
F Cashew	522	1	2	2	2	x 50gm
G Lichen	523	1	1	2	2	x 50gm

NEEDLES

1 pair 3¼mm (no 10) (US 3) needles
1 pair 4mm (no 8) (US 6) needles
3¼mm (no 10) (US 3) circular needle
1 yarn holder

EXTRAS – 1 decorative kilt pin x 00414

TENSION

23 sts and 27 rows to 10 cm measured over pattern using 4mm (US 6) needles.

SPECIAL ABBREVIATIONS

MB = (K1, P1, K1) all into next st, turn, P3, turn, K3, turn, P3, turn, sl 1, K2tog, psso.

BACK

Using 3¼mm (US 3) needles and yarn A cast on 111 [123: 137: 151] sts.
Row 1 (RS): P0 [0: 1: 2], *K3, P3, rep from * to last 3 [3: 4: 5] sts, K3, P0 [0: 1: 2].
Row 2: K0 [0: 1: 2], *P3, K3, rep from * to last 3 [3: 4: 5] sts, P3, K0 [0: 1: 2].
These 2 rows form rib.
Cont in rib for a further 26 rows, ending with RS facing for next row.
Change to 4mm (US 6) needles.
Beg and ending rows as indicated, using the **fairisle** technique as described on the information page and repeating the 28 row patt

Key

- □ A
- ■ B
- □ C — K on RS, P on WS
- ▨ D
- ■ E
- ▣ F — MB
- ▨ G

repeat throughout, cont in patt from chart as folls:
Work 52 [54: 58: 60] rows, ending with RS facing for next row. (Back should meas 29 [30: 31: 32] cm.)

Shape for sleeves
Keeping patt correct, inc 1 st at each end of next and 2 foll 4th rows, then on foll 3 alt rows, then on foll 4 rows, ending with **WS** facing for next row. 131 [143: 157: 171] sts.
Cast on 3 sts at beg of next 4 rows. 143 [155: 169: 183] sts.
Cont straight until armhole meas 23 [24: 25: 26] cm **from last set of cast-on sts**, ending with RS facing for next row.

Shape shoulders and back neck
Cast off 17 [19: 21: 23] sts at beg of next 2 rows. 109 [117: 127: 137] sts.
Next row (RS): Cast off 17 [19: 21: 23] sts, patt until there are 21 [23: 25: 28] sts on right needle and turn, leaving rem sts on a holder.
Work each side of neck separately.
Cast off 4 sts at beg of next row.
Cast off rem 17 [19: 21: 24] sts.
With RS facing, rejoin yarns to rem sts, cast off centre 33 [33: 35: 35] sts, patt to end.
Complete to match first side, reversing shapings.

LEFT FRONT
Using 3¼mm (US 3) needles and yarn A cast on 81 [87: 94: 101] sts.
Row 1 (RS): P0 [0: 1: 2], *K3, P3, rep from * to last 3 sts, K3.
Row 2: *P3, K3, rep from * to last 3 [3: 4: 5] sts, P3, K0 [0: 1: 2].
These 2 rows form rib.
Cont in rib for a further 26 rows, ending with RS facing for next row.
Change to 4mm (US 6) needles.

Shape front slope
Beg and ending rows as indicated, cont in patt from chart as folls:
Dec 1 st at end of next and foll 25 [24: 22: 20] alt rows, then on 0 [1: 3: 4] foll 4th rows.
55 [61: 68: 76] sts.

Work 1 [1: 1: 3] rows, ending with RS facing for next row. (Left front should now match back to beg of sleeve shaping.)

Shape for sleeve
Keeping patt correct, inc 1 st at beg of next and 2 foll 4th rows, then on foll 3 alt rows, then on foll 4 rows **and at same time dec** 1 st at front slope edge of next [3rd: 3rd: next] and every foll 4th row. 60 [66: 73: 81] sts.
Work 1 row, ending with RS facing for next row.
Cast on 3 sts at beg of next and foll alt row **and at same time** dec 1 st at front slope edge of next [3rd: 3rd: next] row. 65 [71: 78: 86] sts.
Dec 1 st at front slope edge **only** on 2nd [4th: 4th: 2nd] and every foll 4th row until 51 [57: 63: 70] sts rem.
Cont straight until left front matches back to beg of shoulder shaping, ending with RS facing for next row.

Shape shoulder
Cast off 17 [19: 21: 23] sts at beg of next and foll alt row.
Work 1 row.
Cast off rem 17 [19: 21: 24] sts.

RIGHT FRONT
Using 3¼mm (US 3) needles and yarn A cast on 81 [87: 94: 101] sts.
Row 1 (RS): *K3, P3, rep from * to last 3 [3: 4: 5] sts, K3, P0 [0: 1: 2].
Row 2: K0 [0: 1: 2], *P3, K3, rep from * to last 3 sts, P3.
These 2 rows form rib.
Cont in rib for a further 26 rows, ending with RS facing for next row.
Change to 4mm (US 6) needles.

Shape front slope
Beg and ending rows as indicated, cont in patt from chart as folls:
Dec 1 st at beg of next and foll 25 [24: 22: 20] alt rows, then on 0 [1: 3: 4] foll 4th rows.
55 [61: 68: 76] sts.
Complete to match left front, reversing shapings.

MAKING UP
Press as described on the information page.
Join both shoulder seams using back stitch, or mattress stitch if preferred.

Front band
With RS facing, using 3¼mm (US 3) circular needle and yarn A, beg and ending at cast-on edges, pick up and knit 24 sts up right front opening edge to beg of front slope shaping, 140 [146: 151: 154] sts up right front slope, 41 [41: 43: 43] sts from back, 140 [146: 151: 154] sts down left front slope to beg of front slope shaping, then 24 sts down left front opening edge.
369 [381: 393: 399] sts.
Row 1 (WS): P3, *K3, P3, rep from * to end.
Row 2: K3, *P3, K3, rep from * to end.
These 2 rows form rib.
Work in rib for a further 3 rows, ending with RS of body facing for next row.
Row 6 (RS): Rib 205 [211: 218: 221], wrap next st (by slipping next st on left needle onto right needle, taking yarn to opposite side of work between needles and then slipping same st back onto left needle – when working back across wrapped sts work the st and the wrapped loop tog as one st) and turn.
Row 7: Rib 41 [41: 43: 43], wrap next st and turn.
Row 8: Rib 49 [49: 51: 51], wrap next st and turn.
Row 9: Rib 57 [57: 59: 59], wrap next st and turn.
Row 10: Rib 65 [65: 67: 67], wrap next st and turn.
Row 11: Rib 73 [73: 75: 75], wrap next st and turn.
Cont in this way, working 8 more sts on every row before wrapping next st and turning, until the foll row has been worked:
Next row (WS of body): Rib 273 [289: 291: 307], wrap next st and turn.
Next row: Rib 283 [299: 301: 317], wrap next st and turn.
Next row: Rib 293 [309: 311: 327], wrap next st and turn.
Next row: Rib 303 [319: 321: 337], wrap next st and turn.
Next row: Rib 313 [329: 331: 347], wrap next st

and turn.

Next row: Rib to end.

Work in rib across all sts for a further 28 rows, ending with **WS** of body facing for next row.

Cast off in rib (on **WS**).

Armhole borders (both alike)

With RS facing, using 3¼mm (US 3) needles and yarn A, pick up and knit 117 [123: 129: 135] sts evenly along straight row-end edge of armhole.

Work in rib as given for front band for 7 rows, ending with RS facing for next row.

Cast off in rib.

See information page for finishing instructions.

Fasten fronts with kilt pin as in photograph.

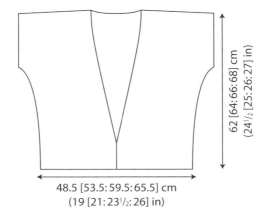

62 [64: 66: 68] cm
(24½ [25: 26: 27] in)

48.5 [53.5: 59.5: 65.5] cm
(19 [21: 23½: 26] in)

Main image page 40

Penny Beanie

YARN

			1-3	3-5	years
RYC Cashsoft DK and Cashsoft Baby DK					
A Baby	Horseradish	801	1	1	x 50gm
B DK	Bloom	520	1	1	x 50gm
C DK	Glacier	504	1	1	x 50gm
D DK	Ballad Blue	508	1	1	x 50gm
E DK	Lime	509	1	1	x 50gm
F DK	Sweet	501	1	1	x 50gm
G DK	Mirage	503	1	1	x 50gm

NEEDLES

1 pair 4mm (no 8) (US 6) needles

TENSION

23 sts and 27 rows to 10 cm measured over pattern using 4mm (US 6) needles.

SPECIAL ABBREVIATIONS

MB = (K1, P1, K1) all into next st, turn, P3, turn, K3, turn, P3, turn, sl 1, K2tog, psso.

BEANIE

Using 4mm (US 6) needles and yarn A cast on 110 [118] sts.
Row 1 (RS): K2, *P2, K2, rep from * to end.
Row 2: P2, *K2, P2, rep from * to end.
These 2 rows form rib.
Cont in rib for a further 2 rows, dec 1 st at end of last row and ending with RS facing for next row.
109 [117] sts.
Beg and ending rows as indicated and **noting that chart row 1 is a WS row**, cont in patt from chart until chart row 28 [34] has been completed, ending with RS facing for next row.
Break off contrasts and cont using yarn A only.
Next row (WS): Purl.

Shape crown

Row 1 (RS): *K2, K2tog, rep from * to last st, K1.
82 [88] sts.
Row 2 and every foll alt row: Purl.
Rows 3 and 5: Knit.
Row 7: *K1, K2tog, rep from * to last st, K1.
55 [59] sts.
Row 9: Knit.
Row 11: *K2tog, rep from * to last st, K1.
28 [30] sts.
Row 13: *K2tog, rep from * to end.
Row 14: Purl.
Break yarn and thread through rem 14 [15] sts.
Pull up tight and fasten off securely.

MAKING UP

Press as described on the information page.
Join back seam using back stitch, or mattress stitch if preferred.

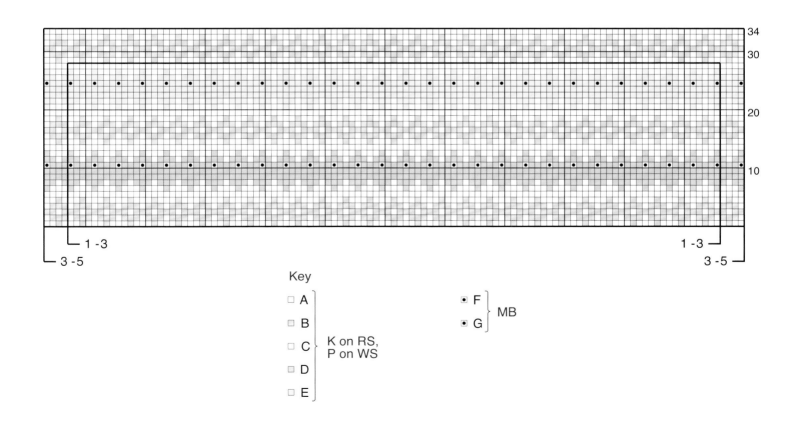

Key

- □ A
- ▨ B
- □ C } K on RS, P on WS
- ▨ D
- ▨ E
- ▪ F } MB
- ▪ G

Main image page 41

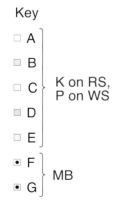

Penny Jacket

YARN

			1-2	2-3	3-4	4-5	years
To fit chest			56	58	61	64	cm
			22	23	24	25	in

RYC Cashsoft DK and Cashsoft Baby DK

A	Baby	Horseradish	801	3	3	3	4	x 50gm
B	DK	Bloom	520	1	2	2	2	x 50gm
C	DK	Glacier	504	1	1	1	1	x 50gm
D	DK	Ballad Blue	508	1	1	1	1	x 50gm
E	DK	Lime	509	1	1	1	1	x 50gm
F	DK	Sweet	501	1	1	1	1	x 50gm
G	DK	Mirage	503	1	1	1	1	x 50gm

NEEDLES

1 pair 3¼mm (no 10) (US 3) needles
1 pair 4mm (no 8) (US 6) needles
1 yarn holder

BUTTONS – 6 x 00400

TENSION

23 sts and 27 rows to 10 cm measured over pattern using 4mm (US 6) needles.

SPECIAL ABBREVIATIONS

MB = (K1, P1, K1) all into next st, turn, P3, turn, K3, turn, P3, turn, sl 1, K2tog, psso.

BACK

Using 3¼mm (US 3) needles and yarn A cast on 71 [75: 79: 83] sts.
Row 1 (RS): K1 [0: 0: 1], P3 [0: 2: 3], *K3, P3, rep from * to last 1 [3: 5: 1] sts, K1 [3: 3: 1], P0 [0: 2: 0].
Row 2: P1 [0: 0: 1], K3 [0: 2: 3], *P3, K3, rep from * to last 1 [3: 5: 1] sts, P1 [3: 3: 1], K0 [0: 2: 0].
These 2 rows form rib.
Cont in rib for a further 8 rows, ending with RS facing for next row.
Change to 4mm (US 6) needles.
Beg and ending rows as indicated, using the **fairisle** technique as described on the information page and repeating the 28 row patt

repeat throughout, cont in patt from chart as folls:
Cont straight until back meas 16 [17: 19: 20] cm, ending with RS facing for next row.
Shape armholes
Keeping patt correct, cast off 3 sts at beg of next 2 rows. 65 [69: 73: 77] sts.
Dec 1 st at each end of next 3 rows.
59 [63: 67: 71] sts.
Cont straight until armhole meas 14 [15: 15: 16] cm, ending with RS facing for next row.
Shape shoulders and back neck
Next row (RS): Cast off 9 [10: 10: 11] sts, patt until there are 10 [11: 12: 13] sts on right needle and turn, leaving rem sts on a holder.
Work each side of neck separately.
Dec 1 st at beg of next row.
Cast off rem 9 [10: 11: 12] sts.
With RS facing, rejoin yarns to rem sts, cast off centre 21 [21: 23: 23] sts, patt to end.
Complete to match first side, reversing shapings.

LEFT FRONT

Using 3¼mm (US 3) needles and yarn A cast on 36 [38: 40: 42] sts.
Row 1 (RS): K1 [0: 0: 1], P3 [0: 2: 3], *K3, P3, rep from * to last 2 sts, K2.

Key

A
B
C — K on RS, P on WS
D
E

F] MB
G

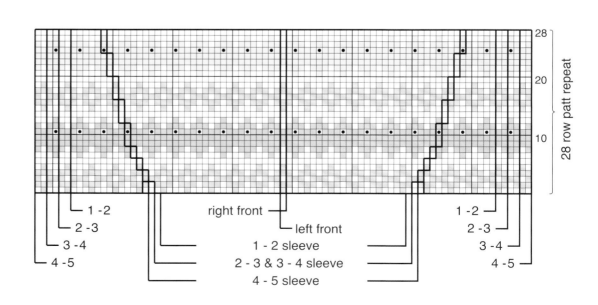

1 -2
2 -3
3 -4
4 -5

right front
left front
1 - 2 sleeve
2 - 3 & 3 - 4 sleeve
4 - 5 sleeve

1 -2
2 -3
3 -4
4 -5

28 row patt repeat

Row 2: P2, K3, *P3, K3, rep from * to last 1 [3: 5: 1] sts, P1 [3: 3: 1], K0 [0: 2: 0].
These 2 rows form rib.
Cont in rib for a further 8 rows, ending with RS facing for next row.
Change to 4mm (US 6) needles.
Beg and ending rows as indicated, cont in patt from chart until left front matches back to beg of armhole shaping, ending with RS facing for next row.
Shape armhole
Keeping patt correct, cast off 3 sts at beg of next row. 33 [35: 37: 39] sts.
Work 1 row.
Dec 1 st at armhole edge of next 3 rows.
30 [32: 34: 36] sts.
Cont straight until 5 [5: 7: 7] rows less have been worked than on back to beg of shoulder shaping, ending with **WS** facing for next row.
Shape neck
Keeping patt correct, cast off 9 sts at beg of next row. 21 [23: 25: 27] sts.
Dec 1 st at neck edge of next 3 rows, then on foll 0 [0: 1: 1] alt row. 18 [20: 21: 23] sts.
Work 1 row, ending with RS facing for next row.
Shape shoulder
Cast off 9 [10: 10: 11] sts at beg of next row.
Work 1 row.
Cast off rem 9 [10: 11: 12] sts.

RIGHT FRONT
Using 3¼mm (US 3) needles and yarn A cast on 36 [38: 40: 42] sts.
Row 1 (RS): K2, P3, *K3, P3, rep from * to last 1 [3: 5: 1] sts, K1 [3: 3: 1], P0 [0: 2: 0].
Row 2: P1 [0: 0: 1], K3 [0: 2: 3], *P3, K3, rep from * to last 2 sts, P2.
These 2 rows form rib.
Complete to match left front, reversing shapings.

SLEEVES
Using 3¼mm (US 3) needles and yarn A cast on 41 [43: 43: 45] sts.
Row 1 (RS): P1 [2: 2: 3], *K3, P3, rep from * to last 4 [5: 5: 6] sts, K3, P1 [2: 2: 3].

Row 2: K1 [2: 2: 3], *P3, K3, rep from * to last 4 [5: 5: 6] sts, P3, K1 [2: 2: 3].
These 2 rows form rib.
Cont in rib for a further 8 rows, ending with RS facing for next row.
Change to 4mm (US 6) needles.
Beg and ending rows as indicated, cont in patt from chart, shaping sides by inc 1 st at each end of next and every foll alt [alt: alt: 4th] row to 51 [53: 49: 73] sts, then on every foll 4th [4th: 4th: -] row until there are 65 [69: 69: -] sts, taking inc sts into patt.
Cont straight until sleeve meas 20 [22: 24: 27] cm, ending with RS facing for next row.
Shape top
Keeping patt correct, cast off 3 sts at beg of next 2 rows.
59 [63: 63: 67] sts.
Dec 1 st at each end of next and foll 2 alt rows, then on foll row, ending with RS facing for next row.
Cast off rem 51 [55: 55: 59] sts.

MAKING UP
Press as described on the information page.
Join both shoulder seams using back stitch, or mattress stitch if preferred.
Neckband
With RS facing, using 3¼mm (US 3) needles and yarn A, beg and ending at front opening edges,

pick up and knit 17 [17: 19: 19] sts up right side of neck, 23 [23: 25: 25] sts from back, then 17 [17: 19: 19] sts down left side of neck.
57 [57: 63: 63] sts.
Row 1 (WS): P3, *K3, P3, rep from * to end.
Row 2: K3, *P3, K3, rep from * to end.
These 2 rows form rib.
Work in rib for a further 4 rows, ending with **WS** facing for next row.
Cast off in rib (on **WS**).
Button band
With RS facing, using 3¼mm (US 3) needles and yarn A, pick up and knit 75 [81: 81: 87] sts evenly down left front opening edge, from top of neckband to cast-on edge.
Work in rib as given for neckband for 6 rows, ending with **WS** facing for next row.
Cast off in rib (on **WS**).
Buttonhole band
Work to match button band, picking up sts up right front opening edge and with the addition of 6 buttonholes in row 4 worked as folls:
Row 4 (RS): Rib 2 [3: 3: 3], *yrn, work 2 tog (to make a buttonhole), rib 12 [13: 13: 14], rep from * 4 times more, yrn, work 2 tog (to make 6th buttonhole), rib 1 [1: 1: 2].
See information page for finishing instructions, setting in sleeves using the shallow set-in method.

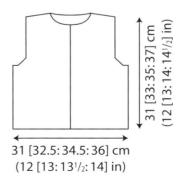

31 [33: 35: 37] cm
(12 [13: 14: 14½] in)

31 [32.5: 34.5: 36] cm
(12 [13: 13½: 14] in)

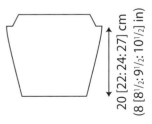

20 [22: 24: 27] cm
(8 [8½: 9½: 10½] in)

Main image page 14

 Zoo

YARN

	0-3	3-6	6-12	12-18 months
To fit chest	41	46	51	56 cm
	16	18	20	22 in

RYC Cashcotton 4 ply

A Cream	900	2	2	2	3	x 50gm
B Cork	904	1	1	1	1	x 50gm
C Sea Foam	903	1	1	1	1	x 50gm

NEEDLES

1 pair 2¾mm (no 12) (US 2) needles
1 pair 3¼mm (no 10) (US 3) needles
2¾mm (no 12) (US 2) circular needle
1 yarn holder

TENSION

28 sts and 36 rows to 10 cm measured over
stocking stitch using 3¼mm (US 3) needles.

BACK

Using 2¾mm (US 2) needles and yarn B cast on
62 [70: 78: 86] sts.
Row 1 (RS): K2, *P2, K2, rep from * to end.
Break off yarn B and join in yarn A.
Row 2: P2, *K2, P2, rep from * to end.

These 2 rows form rib.
Using yarn A **only**, work in rib for a further 10 rows,
inc 1 [1: 0: 0] st at each end of last row and
ending with RS facing for next row.
64 [72: 78: 86] sts.
Change to 3¼mm (US 3) needles.
Using the **fairisle** technique as described on the
information page and beg and ending rows as
indicated, work in patt from chart for lower
border until all 8 rows have been completed,
ending with RS facing for next row.
Break off contrasts and cont using yarn A **only**.**
Beg with a K row, work in st st for 30 [42: 52: 62]
rows, ending with RS facing for next row.
(Back should meas 14 [17: 20: 23] cm.)
Shape armholes
Cast off 5 [6: 6: 7] sts at beg of next 2 rows.
54 [60: 66: 72] sts.
Dec 1 st at each end of next 2 rows, ending with
RS facing for next row. 50 [56: 62: 68] sts.
Using the **fairisle** technique as described on the
information page and beg and ending rows as
indicated, work in patt from chart for upper
border as folls:
Dec 1 st at each end of next and foll 2 alt rows.

44 [50: 56: 62] sts.
Work 2 rows, ending after chart row 7 and with
WS facing for next row.
Beg with a P row, cont in st st using yarn A **only**
until armhole meas 11 [12: 13: 14] cm, ending with
RS facing for next row.
Shape shoulders and back neck
Next row (RS): Cast off 4 [5: 6: 7] sts, K until
there are 6 [7: 8: 9] sts on right needle and turn,
leaving rem sts on a holder.
Work each side of neck separately.
Dec 1 st at neck edge of next row.
Cast off rem 5 [6: 7: 8] sts.
With RS facing, rejoin yarn to rem sts, cast off
centre 24 [26: 28: 30] sts, K to end.
Complete to match first side, reversing shapings.

FRONT

Work as given for back to **.
Beg with a K row, work in st st for 2 [8: 12: 18] rows,
ending with RS facing for next row.
Place elephant chart
Next row (RS): K11 [15: 18: 22], work next 42 sts
as row 1 of chart for elephant, K to end.
Next row: P11 [15: 18: 22], work next 42 sts as

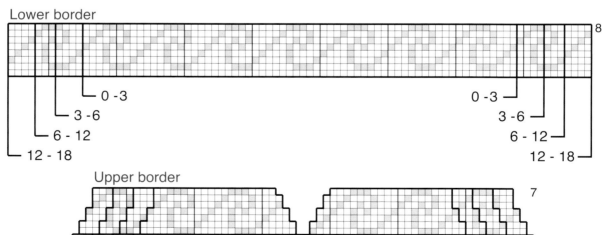

Lower border

8

0 -3
3 -6
6 - 12
12 - 18

0 -3
3 -6
6 - 12
12 - 18

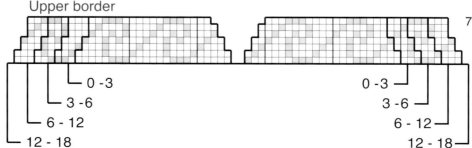

Upper border

7

0 -3
3 -6
6 - 12
12 - 18

0 -3
3 -6
6 - 12
12 - 18

Key

☐ A

☐ B

☐ C

Elephant chart

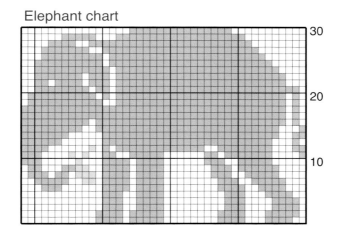

30

20

10

row 2 of chart for elephant, P to end.
These 2 rows set position of chart with edge sts
in yarn A.

0-3 months only

Cont as set until chart row 28 has been
completed, ending with RS facing for next row.

Shape armholes

Cast off 5 [-: -: -] sts at beg of next 2 rows.
54 [-: -: -] sts.
Break off contrasts and cont using yarn A **only**.

3-6, 6-12 and 12-18 months only

Cont as set until all 30 rows of chart have been
completed, ending with RS facing for next row.
Break off contrasts and cont using yarn A **only**.
Beg with a K row, work in st st for 4 [10: 14] rows,
ending with RS facing for next row.

Shape armholes

Cast off - [6: 6: 7] sts at beg of next 2 rows.
- [60: 66: 72] sts.

All sizes

Dec 1 st at each end of next 2 rows, ending with
RS facing for next row. 50 [56: 62: 68] sts.

Divide for neck

Using the **fairisle** technique as described on the
information page and beg and ending rows as
indicated, work in patt from chart for upper
border as folls:

Next row (RS): K2tog, K22 [25: 28: 31] and turn,
leaving rem sts on a holder.
Work each side of neck separately.
Dec 1 st at neck edge of 2nd and foll 2 alt rows
and at same time dec 1 st at armhole edge of 2nd
and foll alt row, ending after chart row 7 and with
WS facing for next row. 18 [21: 24: 27] sts.
Beg with a P row, cont in st st using yarn A **only**
as folls:
Dec 1 st at neck edge only on 2nd and foll 6 [6:
7: 7] alt rows, then on every foll 4th row until
9 [11: 13: 15] sts rem.
Cont straight until front matches back to beg
of shoulder shaping, ending with RS facing for
next row.

Shape shoulder

Cast off 4 [5: 6: 7] sts at beg of next row.
Work 1 row.
Cast off rem 5 [6: 7: 8] sts.
With RS facing, rejoin yarn to rem sts, K2tog and
slip this st onto a holder, K to last 2 sts, K2tog.
Complete to match first side, reversing shapings.

MAKING UP

Press as described on the information page.

Join both shoulder seams using back stitch, or
mattress stitch if preferred.

Neckband

With RS facing, using 2¾mm (US 2) circular
needle and yarn A, pick up and knit 36 [40:
44: 48] sts down left side of neck, K st from front
holder and mark this st with a coloured thread,
pick up and knit 36 [40: 44: 48] sts up right side
of neck, then 26 [30: 30: 34] sts from back.
99 [111: 119: 131] sts.

Round 1 (RS): (K2, P2) 8 [9: 10: 11] times, K2,
K2tog, K marked st, K2tog tbl, P2, *K2, P2, rep
from * to end.
This round sets position of rib.
Keeping rib correct as now set, cont as folls:

Round 2: Rib to within 2 sts of marked st, K2tog,
K marked st, K2tog tbl, rib to end.

Rounds 3 to 5: As round 2. 89 [101: 109: 121] sts.
Break off yarn A and join in yarn B.

Round 6: As round 2.
Cast off in rib, still decreasing either side of
marked st as before.

Armhole borders (both alike)

With RS facing, using 3¼mm (US 3) needles and
yarn A, pick up and knit 66 [74: 82: 90] sts evenly
all round armhole edge.
Beg with row 2, work in rib as given for back for
6 rows, ending with **WS** facing for next row.
Break off yarn A and join in yarn B.
Work in rib for 1 row more.
Cast off in rib.
See information page for finishing instructions.

26 [30:34:38] cm
(10 [12: 13½:15] in)

23 [25.5: 28: 30.5] cm
(9 [10: 11: 12] in)

sizing guide

- Our sizing now conforms to standard clothing sizes. Therefore if you buy a standard size 12 in clothing, then our size 12 or Medium patterns will fit you perfectly.

- Dimensions in the charts below are body measurements, not garment dimensions, therefore please refer to the measuring guide to help you to determine which is the best size for you to knit.

STANDARD SIZING GUIDE FOR WOMEN

UK SIZE	8	10	12	14	16	18	20	22	
USA Size	6	8	10	12	14	16	18	20	
EUR Size	34	36	38	40	42	44	46	48	
To fit bust	32	34	36	38	40	42	44	46	inches
	82	87	92	97	102	107	112	117	cm
To fit waist	24	26	28	30	32	34	36	38	inches
	61	66	71	76	81	86	91	96	cm
To fit hips	34	6	38	40	42	44	46	48	inches
	87	92	97	102	107	112	117	122	cm

CASUAL SIZING GUIDE FOR WOMEN

As there are some designs that are intended to fit more generously, we have introduced our casual sizing guide. The designs that fall into this group can be recognised by the size range: Small, Medium, Large & Xlarge. Each of these sizes cover two sizes from the standard sizing guide, ie. Size S will fit sizes 8/10, size M will fit sizes 12/14 and so on. The sizing within this chart is also based on the larger size within the range, ie. M will be based on size 14.

UK SIZE	S	M	L	XL	
DUAL SIZE	8/10	12/14	16/18	20/22	
To fit bust	32 – 34	36 – 38	40 – 42	44 – 46	inches
	82 – 87	92 - 97	102 – 107	112 – 117	cm
To fit waist	24 – 26	28 – 30	32 – 34	36 – 38	inches
	61 – 66	71 – 76	81 – 86	91 – 96	cm
To fit hips	34 – 36	38 – 40	42 – 44	46 – 48	inches
	87 – 92	97 – 102	107 – 112	117 – 122	cm

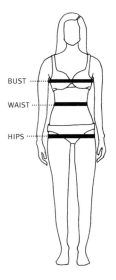

BUST ·······

WAIST ·······

HIPS ·······

MEASURING GUIDE

For maximum comfort and to ensure the correct fit when choosing a size to knit, please follow the tips below when checking your size.

Measure yourself close to your body, over your underwear and don't pull the tape measure too tight!

Bust/chest – measure around the fullest part of the bust/chest and across the shoulder blades.

Waist – measure around the natural waistline, just above the hip bone.

Hips – measure around the fullest part of the bottom.

If you don't wish to measure yourself, note the size of a favourite jumper that you like the fit of. Our sizes are now comparable to the clothing sizes from the major high street retailers, so if your favourite jumper is a size Medium or size 12, then our casual size Medium and standard size 12 should be approximately the same fit.

To be extra sure, measure your favourite jumper and then compare these measurements with the size diagram given at the end of the individual instructions.

Finally, once you have decided which size is best for you, please ensure that you achieve the tension required for the design you wish to knit. Remember if your tension is too loose, your garment will be bigger than the pattern size and you may use more yarn. If your tension is too tight, your garment could be smaller than the pattern size and you will have yarn left over. Furthermore if your tension is incorrect, the handle of your fabric will be too stiff or floppy and will not fit properly. It really does make sense to check your tension before starting every project.